Return to Rest

Praying Through the Psalms
by Katie Holt

Return to Rest: Praying Through the Psalms is a copyrighted material and may not be reproduced or transmitted in any form or by any means, electronic or mechanical, including photocopying and recording, or by any information storage or retrieval system.

ISBN -13: 978-1722105075

To order additional copies of this resource visit www.katieholt.net to order online.

To purchase the accompanying video segments, visit www.katieholt.net to order online.

Dedication

To my amazing husband, Andy, thank you for all your love and support. Your encouragement and affirmation along this journey have been invaluable to me; not to mention the many times you held down the fort so I could have quiet moments away to work.

To my children, Lydia, Alex, Bret, Colin, and Briana, you have been both the reason I've needed to so faithfully stay in my resting place and the embodiment of that rest in every smile, hug, kiss, song, prayer, and deep well of blessing you have been in my life.

To my Girls, Luciana, Wendy, Juvon, and Melissa, you have been my rock, accountability, encouragement, sounding board, joy, and the beautiful expression of God's love and faithfulness in my life. Thank you for all you have contributed to this study.

Table of Contents

Introduction……………………………………………………………4

Chapter 1: Return to Rest………………………………………6

Chapter 2: Know That I Am……………………………………… 30

Chapter 3: I Will Complain…………………………………52

Chapter 4: Nevertheless…………………………………………75

Chapter 5: Teach Me Your ways ………………………………100

Chapter 6: Contend………………………………………………118

Chapter 7: Light Up My Darkness……………………………136

A Note for Bible Study Leaders…………………………………160

Introduction

A few years ago, I stumbled upon Dietrich Bonhoeffer's book *Meditations on Psalms*. I was completely wrecked by this book and by Bonhoeffer himself. I immediately started the book over once I finished it. I read it three times in a row before it finally dawned on me that maybe one reason I loved this book so much was because of the actual Psalms! I thought maybe I should start reading them. Thus, began my own journey of reading and praying through the Psalms. There is just something about them that I can connect with on every emotional level. I relate to David because of how emotional he was and how expressive he was about his emotions. I am a very expressive person, very passionate, and just overall very loud. I cannot be sure, but I think David was loud. That is probably the real reason his parents sent him off alone in the wilderness to shepherd the sheep.

I connect with the Psalms so much, because, besides just David's emotional transparency, you see Papa's (God). I love turning to a chapter in the Psalms and experiencing the Lord's feelings. I have struggled for a long time with letting myself feel anything expect a holy Christian zeal, an overwhelming joy and thankfulness, and deep compassion or sorrow for the lost souls who do not know my Jesus or Papa's love. Some of you may be wondering what is so wrong with that, isn't that all the emotions there is? Well that is what I believed for a while too but y'all, that gets exhausting! Only basically ever feeling glad all the time?! No one can sustain that for too long without driving their husbands and kids crazy. Trust me! I had learned to squash any other feeling because no one else could handle it. I also learned to suppress feelings if they made me feel guilty or like a bad Christian. What I have learned since, in part because of the Psalms, in addition to a lot of inner-healing, counseling, and prayer, is that it is ok to feel other things too.

It is ok to feel anger when someone hurts you. It is ok to feel sadness about unfortunate circumstances completely outside of your control. It does not make you a bad Christian, an ungrateful or thankless Christian, or an angry person to feel your feelings. The biggest break-through for me came when I started learning how to feel my feelings by learning how God feels His. We see those feelings BIG in the book of Psalms. I have learned how to pray through these difficult seasons and negative feelings and even rejoice through the Psalms. I believe every single psalm can be relatable and used as a tool to pray similar to how the Lord's Prayer can be used.

For those skeptics out there, I will quote Edwin Robertson who edited and translated Bonhoeffer's book *Meditations of Psalms*. From the Prologue, "Those who objected that some psalms cannot be prayed with sincerity because the Christian conscience rebelled against what they said or because they could not understand them, met a blunt reply [from Bonhoeffer]: 'The only way to understand the Psalms is on your knees, the whole congregation praying the words of the Psalms with all its strength.' And to those who complained that they cannot pray what they do not understand, the equally blunt reply: 'How can you understand what you have not prayed? It is not our prayer that interprets the Psalms but the Psalms that interpret our prayers.' For Bonhoeffer, as for Martin Luther, the Psalms were both the Word of God and the words of men. The Psalter is both the prayer book of the Church and the prayer of God in Holy Scripture. Luther believed that you could hear the voice of Christ in every psalm- praying with us and for us."

I guess I am in pretty good company when I say I believe the Psalms are both the voice of God and the voice of men. Do I think David had the tendency to exaggerate, to be overly emotional or dramatic? Yes! But therein lies the beauty of the Psalms because I believe that God is also emotional and dare I say even dramatic! Look in creation and tell me He does not have a flare for the ostentatious, absurd, weird, dramatic, and incredible. I mean, He created me after all!

So, when you brush up against a psalm that you do not understand, or that does not apply to your situation, or that you perhaps do not agree with because you think David was off his rocker, do not dismiss it and move on. Remember that someone, somewhere is struggling with this very thing and maybe you are reading that psalm because you are supposed to intercede for them.

This study can be done individually, as a small group, or as a women's Bible study with several small groups all working through it together. You will find throughout the lessons that I ask you to read certain Scriptures. I personally prefer to read and teach from the New American Standard Bible.

I am looking forward to taking this journey through Psalms with you. There is a psalm for every type of situation, every emotion, every up and down, every mountain, and every valley. At the end of each lesson I will share with you one of my favorite psalms and how I pray it. In these prayers, with the exception of changing some pronouns, I stay almost word for word with Scripture using the New American Standard Bible, The Message Bible, and the New Living Translation Bible. I do hope you will allow me some liberties but trust that I stayed true to the psalms. I wrote them as I have prayed them many, many times. I hope you will join me in praying or meditating on them.

At the beginning of each week I will give you a psalm to work on memorizing. There is something really amazing that happens when you take a chapter apart and say it over and over and over and over and memorize. It seeps in to all the little cracks of your soul and it brings LIFE! I know it will be a challenge for many of you but give it a try and work at memorizing at least one chapter by the end of this study. You will not regret it.

Chapter 1

Return to Rest

Notes:

Small Group Questions:

1) Is the concept of a "resting place" completely foreign to you? Discuss with your group what a resting place looks like for you if you have ever experienced being at rest in Him.

2) Share with your group that moment of "conversion" when you submitted your life to Christ and became saved.

3) What does the Lord's "abiding love" mean to you?

4) Is staying in that abiding place of rest difficult for you? Discuss with your group why and what pulls you out of it.

Chapter 1: Return to Rest

Psalm 61 holds a special place in my heart. I memorized it with a group of women I met with weekly for 7 years and I still remember it.

Psalm 61 NASB

1 Hear my cry, O God;
 Give heed to my prayer.

2 From the end of the earth I call to You when my heart is faint;
 Lead me to the rock that is higher than I.

3 For You have been a refuge for me,
 A tower of strength against the enemy.

4 Let me dwell in Your tent forever;
 Let me take refuge in the shelter of Your wings.

Selah.

5 For You have heard my vows, O God;
 You have given me the inheritance of those who fear Your name.

6 You will prolong the king's life;
 His years will be as many generations.

7 He will abide before God forever;
 Appoint lovingkindness and truth that they may preserve him.

8 So I will sing praise to Your name forever,
 That I may pay my vows day by day.

Return to Rest May 18th 2020

Lesson 1

Welcome to Week 1, Lesson 1! This is my first time writing a Bible study and of course it would be on a topic like rest. I had the most difficulty writing this chapter because this is the hardest one for me to practice what I preach. If I have learned anything from my life thus far, from my studies on this subject, and from writing this book, it is that rest does not come from anything we do but from what God does in us. You cannot strive to rest. You cannot try to rest. You cannot determine to do it or set an alarm to schedule it, or create the space, and make yourself rest. Sure, you can do things like get a massage or take a bubble bath to relax your body, but all the bubbles in the world are not going to make your soul enter rest. He is the source of every good thing we have in this life: love, joy, hope, faith, peace, security, and **rest**. Rest only comes from Him, through Him, and by Him.

If you have heard me speak on this topic then you know I learned this the hard way. One day when I was trying to rest Papa whispered to my heart, "Stop 'trying' to rest. Peace and rest are a natural consequence of relationship with Me. You will fall into rest when you simply abide."

Read Psalm 116:1-7

Funny thing about that word *return* in verse 7 is that you cannot return to something unless you leave it in the first place. Do you ever find yourself wandering out of your place of rest? It is so easy to do. We live in a world full of distractions. And pain. We often think the easiest way to get over our pain is to avoid it. I have spent a lot of time avoiding mine. I was in so much denial about the pain caused by my past that I was in denial that I was even in denial! The fact that I just used the word *denial* three times in a sentence shows just how far I have come!

The problem with avoidance and denial is that it is the quickest way out of our resting place. It takes a lot of effort and emotional energy to hide from reality, squash down our feelings, and ignore our pain. That means you are doing the complete opposite of resting.

What keeps you from your resting place? Like David, is it fear? Or sadness (v3)? Or something else? Get quiet for a moment and take inventory of your soul. Relax your body and breathe and allow any *unrest* to surface.

List anything that is bothering you right now.

WORK LIFE - feelings of Scared & Confused, as i feel like i don't know where I am supposed to be or what I am supposed to be doing. Struggling to find my purpose.

It seems one of the ways I am easily pulled out of my resting place is through worry about others, specifically comparison. I worry about their actions and how they will affect me, about what they have, and I do not, and about what they might have said about me to someone else. I worry about what they really think about me.

Read Psalm 37:1, 7 and write what David calls this kind of worry.

Don't worry about the wicked or envy those who do wrong.
Be still in the presence of the Lord and wait patiently for him to act.

Do you struggle with "fretting" too? List the people and/or situation you are fretting over now.

Work, Marriage, worry about my child.

Always fret/worry about what people think of me.

I think David had a point in Psalm 116:6 when he said, "the Lord preserves the simple". That means He *protects*, *keeps*, or *guards* the *open minded*. I spent so much of my time keeping my mind completely shut to my pain to try and protect myself that I could not be open minded to any gifts of healing or freedom the Lord had to offer. I had to maintain a death grip on the lid storing all my suffering. Our society teaches that being simple, open minded, or vulnerable is bad. That is because in our culture people are not safe. They do not know they have a resting place, so they have to be on guard at all times. Anyone who is not that way is seen as weak. The word "simple" now has a negative connotation to it, but the word "simple" from Psalm 116:6 comes from the translated Hebrew word "pthiy" defined as "the open-minded." In other words, those who make space for God in their hearts and minds allow Him to protect them and fill them. It reminds me of what the Lord spoke to me, "you fall into rest when you *simply* abide."

David said he found distress and sorrow; he was brought low. When we feel brought low by stress or sorrow this is not the time to pack away our feelings, ignore our heartache, allow guilt and shame to separate us from God, or to be closed off to His grace. This is the time we must be like David in Psalm 116:4 and call upon the name of the Lord, "O Lord, I beseech You, save my life!" He is gracious. He is compassionate. When we are open to Him He will save us!

Read Psalm 116:1-4 again.

Handwritten: I love the Lord because he hears my voice and my prayer for mercy. Because he bends down to listen, I will pray as long as I have breath! Death wrapped its ropes around me, the terrors of the Grave overtook me, I saw only trouble & sorrow. Then I called on the name of the Lord: "Please Lord, Save me!"

The order of these events is so interesting! First David says, one of the reasons he loves God is because God always hears his voice. But in verse 3 he says death and terror surrounded him. So, is it possible to know that God hears you and your cries but still *feel* alone and afraid?

I have similar mixed feelings sometimes about God's ability to hear me when I call out. I know He hears me. I am fully confident of this. But my soul seems to easily forget. Can you relate? *Yes*

Can you remember a time you called out to God and wondered if He heard or if He cared? Write it here.

This past few months (in fact this year) - anxiety re work situation.

How about a time you heard His response right away?

Praying about a neighbor - worried/anxious about our friendship - Then receiving a text straight away & feeling calm within.

Maybe this is why David has to remind his soul to return to rest: because knowing God hears and abiding in Him are two different things. There is a difference between knowing God loves us and hears our cries and actually abiding in His love. Let's walk through this together as we pray this prayer from Psalm 116 and call our souls back to their place of rest.

Lord, I love You because I know you hear my voice and my supplications. Therefore, I shall call upon Your name for as long as I live. Even when fear encompasses me, and I find myself in distress and sorrow I will call upon Your name. You are gracious and righteous; You are compassionate. You preserve the simple. I will trust that when I am brought low You will save me when I cry out to You. Return to rest, O my soul, for the Lord has dealt bountifully with you. You, God, have rescued my soul from death and given me eternal life. I will walk before You in the land of the living. I will call upon the name of the Lord in the presence of all Your people. O Lord, I am Your servant, You have set me free. I will offer up sacrifices of thanksgiving and call upon Your name. Praise the Lord!

Amen

Return to Rest

Lesson 2

In Lesson One we looked at Psalm 116:7. Well, I am not quite done with it. I told you it was one of my favorites after all.

Read Psalm 116:7

Remember that the word "menuchah," the transliterated word for *"rest"* here means an actual *place of rest*. This is the same word used in the well-known chapter of Psalm 23.

Read Psalm 23

Take a guess at which word is the same Hebrew word "menuchah" and write it here.

___

Did you guess the word *quiet* from Psalm 23:2? "He leads me beside *quiet* waters." In Lesson One I discussed with you the importance of telling our soul to return to rest once we have found ourselves in distress or trouble. Maybe you were a bit skeptical of this and I do not blame you. Sometimes it is not so easy and remember, we cannot strive to rest even if we are striving to tell ourselves to rest. This is why I love that the same word "menuchah" for *rest* in Psalm 116:7 is the word *quiet* in Psalm 23.

Write the sentence from Psalm 23:2 that has the word, "quiet" in it.

___

Sometimes we need our Shepherd to lead us back to our place of rest. This is emphasized when we realize that the word for, "lead" in Hebrew, "nahal," can be defined specifically as *bring to a place of rest*. I think David, together with the Holy Spirit, is trying to make a point! As if that was not clear enough the word, "beside" means *over*. It gives the impression of *hovering over* or *coming down into something from above* like sinking down into a pool of water.

So now that you have all the definitions, fill in the blank:

He leads:_____ beside: _____ Place of Rest waters.

How awesome is that?! I wrote "Place of Rest Waters" to show that this rest is actually a place we go. It reminds me of one of my absolute favorite childhood characters, Anne of Green Gables. I think she would approve of the name for the quiet waters. I can just hear her say, "Oh you are far too beautiful, far too still and peaceful. Why, just gazing on your majesty I am filled with awe and delight. I will call you *Place of Rest Waters* from now on."

Have you ever been led by the Shepherd to the pool of quiet waters? Maybe while working through Lesson One you allowed your body and your soul to return to rest for the first time.

If you were as dramatic as our dear Anne how would you describe your place of rest waters? What name would you give this place and why?

Now obviously it is *completely* out of character for me to be quite so dramatic but, IF I had to pick a name for the place of rest I often feel the Lord leading me to it would be *Sweet Waters of Shalom*. I chose it because sinking into that deep pool of Papa's rest means not just being surrounded by His presence and rest for my soul, it means having every empty place *inside* of me filled as well. This is Shalom. Shalom means nothing lost, nothing missing, and nothing broken. Can you imagine sinking down into a pool of warm abiding love and letting it seep down to your bones until you can no longer tell where your skin starts and His love ends?

Circle a definition for Shalom that you wish you could sink into right now:

completeness, soundness, welfare, closeness, favor, health,

perfect peace, prosperity, safety, security, wholeness, wellness, happiness, rest

Write the reason for your choice:

_____

_____

Now take a moment and ask the Shepherd to lead you there again. As you breathe in let all the things causing you stress rise to the surface, feel them unbuckle from your shoulders and as you breathe out allow them to fall. Breathe in and out as many times as it takes until you can imagine going to a beautiful, crystal clear lake, ocean, pond, pool, stream, or whatever type of water makes you feel comfortable. You packed all the stuff you think you will need and like a pack-horse, you have carried it down to the water. Now as you breathe let those things fall one by one until you are left standing there in just your swimsuit.

When I did this exercise with a friend you could tell the freedom she walked in because in her imagination she took a running leap off a dock and cannon-balled into the water. It is not so easy for me. I find myself standing, sometimes for quite a long while, at the water's edge letting the water lap over my toes until I slowly ease my way in. Eventually, I feel myself sinking to the bottom and allowing that stillness to invade my soul. Shalom.

What about you? Are you like my friend? Joyfully, exuberantly entering in to all Papa has for you? Or are you like me, needing to make a slower approach? Or somewhere in between? Why do you think?

_____

_____

Read Psalm 23:2-3 again.

Oh, I love that word *restores*. He restores my soul. I can tell you what it means but first write down what you think it means especially after being led to quiet waters.

      The short definition for the transliterated Hebrew word, "shub" is *to turn back, return, to be brought back*. I asked you in Lesson One if you had found yourself wandering away from your resting place. We talked about how easy it is to simply tell your soul to return. Then we learned that when we cannot do that we have a Good Shepherd who is willing to bring us back Himself. Now could you allow yourself to be fully restored to the woman of God you were created to be? It is no wonder that David was led to the green pastures and the quiet waters first. His soul was fully restored and fully led by God. This is why he could say with confidence, "Even though I walk through the valley of the shadow of death, I fear no evil, for You are with me." God never intended us to walk through these valleys weak and alone. We were never meant to skip the pasture and the pool and head straight for the valley of death! Thankfully, it is never too late no matter what your situation. Even in that valley Papa is there holding your hand and saying, "Hey, let's make a pit stop over at the *Sweet Waters of Shalom*."

      As a mom of five, there have been many times (a day) I feel myself running low. I tell my kids, "I'm about out of patience for this." Or I hear myself tell a friend, "Oh I'm Ok, just so tired." Or "been a long week, running on fumes." Have you ever felt like you are running on empty? How about financially? Living pay check to pay check, constantly hustling to make ends meet is exhausting and stressful! Times like these, I see that blinking gas-can light on the dashboard of my soul, and I feel myself about to crash and burn. What if in these moments we could allow ourselves to fall right back into the arms of our Good Shephard and be brought back to our resting place? What if we could allow Him to carry us into the water and just for a moment feel that "hover" above the still waters? Could we allow ourselves to sink?

Hold your breath, close your eyes, and let your heart say yes as you breathe out this prayer from Psalm 23.

O Lord, You are my Shepherd, with You I don't need a thing. You cause me to rest in green pastures; And when I can't, Lord, bring me back to my quiet, resting waters. Restore my soul. Guide me in paths of righteousness, and when I walk through the valley of the shadow of death, I will fear no evil, for You are with me; Your rod and Your staff, they comfort me. You prepare a table before me in the presence of my enemies; You revive my soul with anointed oil; cause my cup to overflow with blessing. Lord, never stop pursuing me with Your goodness and mercy or Your unfailing love all the days of my life, and I choose to dwell in Your house, Lord forever.

Amen

Return to Rest

Lesson 3

Today we are going to look at Psalm 25 which has two major themes: *teach me Your ways*, and *You have/will save me and defeat my enemies*. Now I am a teacher at heart so it is hard for me to wait but we will save the first theme for a later chapter in this study. For now, read it and see if you can distinguish the two ideas.

Read chapter 25 and list the number for each verse in these two categories:

Teach Me Your Ways   **Salvation/Justice**

You may be wondering what either of these themes have to do with our chapter topic of returning to rest. Well, sometimes we can picture our pain, or our hurt, or our situation in our mind. We can put them in a metaphorical box or bag. We can carry it down to those resting waters we have been talking about. We can even place them before the Lord to completely surrender them. We can sink down into that pool and let Him fill us up and we can come out feeling clean and fully restored. But what happens next? Sometimes we stay there. Our body and spirit go about its business while our soul stays at rest. But if you are like me, sometimes you return to those boxes of problems again and again and again.

We have to dig into those hurts and hash them out with God. If there is anyone we can learn from when it comes to airing out our dirty laundry before the Lord, it is David. One of my goals for this study guide is for you to learn how to use the Psalms as a tool to pray through these hard things and be completely set free.

Read Psalm 25:1 again.

If you put this verse in both categories above then you are correct. I believe it applies to both.

Now, check out some of the definitions from the NAS Concordance for the word "nasah," the Hebrew word for *lift* and as you do mentally insert them into the verse.

To You, O Lord I _____ my soul....

>bear, bring, carry away, ever forgive, found, laid, lift, lifted, offer, put, raise, receive, regard, released, sets, show, supplied, swore, upheaved

Now, look at the definition for "nephesh," the Hebrew word for *soul* and mentally insert them into the verse

To You, O Lord I lift my _____ ....

>living being, life, self, person, desire, passion, appetite, emotion, body, breath, feelings, heart, longing, mind, strength, will, wishes

One thing I like to do with verses like these is to pray through each definition of the word. For example:

To You, O Lord, I **offer** up my **breath** that every word I breathe would bring You glory or praise.

To You, O Lord, I **bring** my **desires**. Shape and mold them to be in alignment with Your desires.

To You, O Lord, I **bear** my **heart**. See all these hurting places? I give them to You.

And let yourself take some liberties, for example:

I **forgive myself** for every way I have fallen short of Your will.

You try. Draw a line from a verb to a noun and pray through it as it applies to you.

To You, O Lord, I _____ my _____.

Verb for Lift	**Noun for Soul**
Bear	Body
Bring	Life
Ever forgive	Desires
Lay	Passions
Lift	Appetite
Offer	Heart
Raise	Strength
Release	Wishes
Set	Emotions
Show	Feelings

This is such a great exercise. And we have only made it to verse 1!

Read Psalm 25:2, 20

None who wait on Him will be ashamed. Shame cannot abide in our resting place. If you feel shame then you are not there yet. Let Him carry you the rest of the way. Release the guilt and shame and receive refuge. Do not let what is in your baggage cause you to feel shame. We all have it, but the point is: God does not want you to carry it. Do not let shame keep you at the water's edge. It is just another place of bondage.

Read 1 John 2:28

There is that word "abide" again. When we abide in Him: stay in our place of rest, dwell in Him our refuge- there is no *try*. There is just *being*. We do not have to try to be a good Christian, therefore we cannot *fail* at being a good Christian. This leaves us free from shame we may experience from failing. All of the ways we fall short of the glory fall off in Him. He fills us with Himself and we are set free.

Read Psalm 25:2 again.

We will talk more about this in later chapters, but I want to point out that David has a habit of praying for, or you could say, cursing his enemies. For today's lesson I believe there is a deeper implication here we can take from this verse. David is saying, "Do not let me be ashamed; do not let my enemies exult over me." In other words, "Do not let me be defeated and left shamed by my enemies."

We know shame is not from God. Who is the only enemy that can make us feel shame?

We may not have a literal castle wall to peer over and see the armies of our enemy like David did. But we most assuredly do have a very real enemy constantly barraging us with every means of assault, trying to shame us.

Take courage by Psalm25:3. Read it now.

When we enter our resting place and wait on the Lord we can trust that He will deal with our enemy. When we try and take matters into our own hands we are only playing into the enemy's schemes. The Kingdom Way is counter to our culture. We gain freedom by submitting ourselves to the will of the Father. We win by waiting and resting. We fail when we try or strive, and we let the enemy win when we let shame keep us from entering our rest.

Let this sink in as you pray through Psalm 25

To You, O Lord, I lift up my soul. O my God, in You I trust, do not let me be ashamed; do not let my enemies exult over me. Indeed, none of those who wait for You will be ashamed; those who deal treacherously without cause will be ashamed. Make me know Your ways, O Lord; teach me Your paths. Lead me in Your truth and teach me, for You are the God of my salvation; for You I wait all day. For Your name's sake, O Lord, pardon my iniquity, for it is great. My eyes are continually toward You, Lord, for You will pluck my feet out of the net. Turn to me and be gracious to me, for I am lonely and afflicted. The troubles of my heart are enlarged; Bring me out of my distresses. Look upon my affliction and my trouble and forgive all my sins. Guard my soul and deliver me; do not let me be ashamed for I take refuge in You. Let integrity and uprightness preserve me, for I wait for You.

Amen

Return to Rest

Lesson 4

Let me get practical. The last three lessons were focused on returning to emotional and spiritual rest. But I want to talk about real, everyday life. I love reading personal development books but if they do not tell me in realistic terms how to actually implement the concepts in practical ways it is basically a waste of time. So how do we physically return to rest and what are the things that pull you away from it?

While I write this, at this very moment, my commitments include:

Wife

Mom of 5

Homeschool mom of 4

Babysitter of my sweet niece

Board of Directors for our homeschool co-op

Bible study leader

Social Skills teacher for a group of ladies from the sober living house I volunteer at

Mom's support group leader

Piano teacher

Author/Speaker

And this is me with a light schedule without listing any of my kids' activities and schedules. As you can see, the easiest way for me to leave my resting place is by *doing*. I tend to overcommit, overdo, get too busy, wear myself out, and allow myself to be exhausted mentally, emotionally, and physically. This is a fine line for me though. If I cut out too many things that are really important to me, that are life giving and that I love to do, I tend to get depressed and sink back into my Netflix addiction.

The only way for me to walk this fine line is to stay centered and focused at my core. I have to devote a solid amount of time to intentionally allowing my soul to return to rest. I always want to lean in to Him no matter what I do but to truly keep my cup full I have to have "quiet time". This is not a new concept in the Christian world, and it looks different for everyone. For me quiet time looks like waking up early and just sitting. Sometimes I drink coffee (who am I kidding, there is always coffee), sometimes I turn on worship music, sometimes I read the Bible, sometimes I pray or meditate, but mostly I just sit. I listen. I wait. I command my soul to be quiet and to return to rest. Remember that the place of rest is in us because He is in us. The source of that rest is not ourselves or anything we can conjure up on our own. We can, however, make our body stop what it is doing and clear our minds to listen and obey Him when He calls. We must work at developing this practice. It does get easier over time. I cannot fully explain how impactful, beneficial, and life changing this commitment has been for me.

Your turn. List your life roles and commitments (feel free to write in the back if you are like me and need more than two lines):

_____

_____

Which commitment draws you out of your resting place the most?

_____

_____

Are you familiar with the term *Self-care*? Oh, the number of women I have counseled, especially moms, who may have heard the term, may even agree with the principle, but still feel guilty when they do something to love themselves. Christian women are especially prone to feeling selfish any time they make anything about them. Ladies, we give and give and give and give. You must take time to give to and love yourself. The advice I usually give to women who have a hard time with this is the same advice that helped me years ago when I read *The Surrendered Wife* by Laura Doyle. She says to list 10 things you love to do that are fun and 10 things you need to do because they make you feel good.

List 10 things you love to do that are just plain fun.

1
2
3
4
5
6
7
8
9
10

Now list 10 that make you feel good after doing them but aren't necessarily fun- like exercising.

1
2
3
4
5
6
7
8
9
10

Now, try and do at least three things total out of those 20 options per day. This has helped me so much from getting too depleted and I have recognized that when I do feel depleted it is because I have not done at least 3 things. I have heard every excuse in the book from busy women who have bought into the lie of the enemy that they do not have time to take care of themselves. You saw my list of commitments. I understand what it means to be busy. If I can make time in my day to do three things off those lists so can you. We make time for what is important. Evaluate where your time is going and make yourself a priority. You are a priority to God. Do not ignore the leading of the Holy Spirit to be filled and cared for.

Read Psalm 37:3-4

The truth is God wants us to enjoy this life. We cannot do that if we are fretting or staying busy all the time. Take time to delight yourself in Him and enjoy the safety and security your Resting Place brings. Verse three literally means when we abide in Him all will be provided. I love another translation for "delight." It means to *luxuriate*. Luxuriate yourself in the Lord. Take that candle-lit bubble bath, get the massage, enjoy an ice cream sundae every now and then, pursue a hobby you have always wanted to do just for fun, or even write that book you have had on your heart for so long! All of these things can be a way to tune in to what our bodies and our souls need. It allows for more opportunities for the Lord to invade and help us return to our resting place.

Pray through this with the help of Psalm 37:

Father, I will trust in You; I will enjoy and do good. I will abide in the resting place you have provided and delight in Your provision I find there. I luxuriate in Your presence; thank you for all the desires You've placed in my heart and I trust that You will be the one to fulfill them. I commit myself to Your way and will trust only in You believing you are faithful to do all You said you would. Thank you for validating my life and giving me Your stamp of approval. I choose to rest in You. I wait patiently on You. I repent of worry and receive forgiveness for all my fretting; I trust You to prosper my way. I will follow Your leading and be happy trusting no matter if I stumble You hold my hand. You are my strength in times of trouble. You are my Help and Deliverer. Deliver me from the wicked and save me because I take refuge only in You. Amen

Return to Rest

Lesson 5

Have you ever heard that saying, "If Momma ain't happy, ain't nobody happy"? I was born and raised in Oklahoma and my husband loves to tease me about my accent. He spent the first 10 years of our marriage helping me learn how to pronounce "ambulance" the correct way instead of saying "ambliance". So, when I say, "if Momma ain't happy, ain't nobody happy." Then *y'all* know I mean *ain't*.

Have you noticed that when you are not abiding in your resting place it affects the people around you? My first four children all started sleeping through the night by ten weeks. I like to say that my fifth baby made up the difference. I do not think I slept more than three hours at a time for nine months. Now imagine having to still function and keep all those kids alive during the day!

I remember driving the car one day after I had just finished squawking at everyone to hurry up and get in the car. Lord knows I was tired, but I was also so angry and ugly in my dealings with my kids. Half way to our destination the Lord arrested my soul when I heard His words on my heart,

> *"What does it mean if all the enemy has to do is steal a few hours of sleep for you to lose yourself?"*

This was not a shaming from God or even really a correction. It was a realization that sleep deprivation became a justification for me to forget the woman of God I was created to be.

The Holy Spirit began to shine His light on truth. What if God could help me? What if He could invade my soul and body and my family and infuse us all with grace? What if I could lean into Him and let Him save me even in this incredibly challenging, sleep deprived time?

I did not experience any dramatic shift in my circumstances. Mary Poppins did not fly in and save me so I could nap. But, the more I practice living out of my resting place the more at peace my inner world becomes which does cause a noticeable shift in our home.

Read Colossians 3:15-17

The word *peace* in verse 15 is translated from the Greek word "eiréné" which means: *to be exempt from rage or havoc or war or turmoil*. Thayer's Greek Lexicon put it this way, *"according to a conception distinctly peculiar to Christianity, 'the tranquil state of a soul assured of its salvation through Christ, and so fearing nothing from God and content with its earthly lot, of whatsoever sort that is.'"* In other words, it means the same concept of rest that we have been talking about this whole chapter.

We can abide in our resting place, we can give out of our resting place, and we can let this place rule in our hearts; indeed, we are called to do so. Not only can we dwell here but, in fact, Christ can dwell here with us (v16).

Read Psalm 132:13-14

Not only is He our resting place, but we are His. We were literally created to be His resting place and He longs to dwell there. The same fulfillment and joy we receive by dwelling in this place of rest He too experiences in us! It is truly wonderful! This communion and relationship are what He longs for and finds mutual satisfaction in. It is what we were created for.

Read Psalm 16:8

The Lord will never leave you. When we have wandered out of our resting place the only thing to do is to return. Whether we make a choice and turn ourselves or we allow Him to carry us back, there is a mental shift that must take place in our minds. It takes intentionality to maintain this relationship with the Father, to continue to dwell. Like David, we must "set the Lord before us."

This may not be that difficult for a lot of you, but some may be struggling. We know guilt and shame do not come from the Lord so drop that right now. Perhaps you are experiencing that warm, gentle, albeit unpleasant, sensation of the Holy Spirit bringing conviction. Not only does a mental shift need to take place, a spiritual one must happen as well. Maybe He is gently reminding you of the sin that caused you to leave your resting place. Do not worry or feel ashamed. You are not alone. We have all done it. Maybe it is an attitude like what I experienced that sleep deprived day. Maybe there is a justification or a prideful posture of believing you are strong enough on your own, that you do not need to rest in Him. Perhaps you are withholding forgiveness from someone else. That one can be so hard to release. Remember that He does not want us to carry ANY of these burdens including the hurt caused by others. Our soul will not be able to enter rest if we continue to hold on to the things that are dragging us down.

Write down any feelings of conviction you may be experiencing. Try to avoid thinking about what YOU will do about it or how you can change. Just write what the Spirit brings to your mind.

_____

_____

The easiest way out of rest is to avoid the conviction of the Holy Spirit. Have you ever tried? David did.

Read Psalm 39:2 and write down what he says happened.

_____

Oh, how I can relate to this! I think to myself, *"Maybe if I do some volunteer work this feeling will go away. Maybe if I do a devotional and put on some worship music, I won't have to deal with this. Maybe I'll exercise and fast and then read a personal development book and then I'll feel better."* And if all else fails I can just disappear in Netflix for a while, so I no longer have to think about it.

Write about a time you have tried to avoid God and His leading to repentance. What is your go-to method of avoidance?

_____

_____

Read Psalm 39:7-8

The fastest, often the *only* path back to rest is through forgiveness and that just means it is through Jesus. It is the reason He died for you in the first place.

Take a moment to write a prayer of repentance. It can be as simple as David's, "deliver me from all my transgressions" or pull out a journal and take your time. Either way, keep going until you can let go of that unrepentant/unforgiveness baggage. It does not belong with you in your resting place. Jesus gave all of Himself so you would not have to carry those things any more. He wants to set you free.

_____

_____

_____

Once you have finished, pray through Psalm 16 and journey back to your resting place.

Preserve me, O God, for I take refuge in You. You are my Lord; I have no good besides You. You are my portion and my first choice. I set you before me, I return to rest because You have taken my hand. I will not be shaken. Fill me with joy and cause my heart to be glad. My soul will dwell securely in my resting place in You. For You will not abandon my soul to hell. Father, make known to me the path of life; in Your presence I receive fullness of joy.

Amen

Chapter 2

Know That I Am

Notes:

Small Group Discussion Questions:

1) Discuss with your group if you have ever experienced a "Nathanael moment" where God told you who you are so you could know Him.

2) Share about a time you have been disappointed in God because He did not meet your expectations.

3) The first absolute truth We learned in this week's lesson about who God is, is that He is God with us. Discuss with your group how that makes you feel.

Chapter 2: Know That I Am

This is a beautiful Psalm and goes perfectly with this week's lesson. Underline all the Biblical truths describing God's character. Each time you read this chapter of Psalms let your soul be reminded of these truths about who He is.

Psalm 100 NASB

1 Shout joyfully to the LORD, all the earth.

2 Serve the LORD with gladness;
Come before Him with joyful singing.

3 Know that the LORD Himself is God;
It is He who has made us, and not we ourselves;
We are His people and the sheep of His pasture.

4 Enter His gates with thanksgiving
And His courts with praise.
Give thanks to Him, bless His name.

5 For the LORD is good;
His lovingkindness is everlasting
And His faithfulness to all generations.

Know That I Am

Lesson 1

      Years ago, the Father started speaking to me to, "Know that I Am." The more I thought and prayed about that, the more I realized that who I thought He was, He was not. I began to see the many cracks in my foundational belief system and the lies I had been believing began to be exposed. At the time there were some immediate changes He wanted to make but this journey still continues to this day. We never fully understand who He is or know Him completely. As we start this next chapter I pray that you would take this opportunity to allow the Father to expose any lies you have believed about His character. I hope you are able to use the Psalm Prayers at the end of each lesson to pray through some of these truths. I pray that He would continue to take you deeper into the depths of I Am. Remember, this is all done in our resting place where unnecessary baggage falls away and He fills us up, restores our souls, and we experience a deeper abiding love than before. Guilt and shame have no place here and as you will see we are not the only ones who need to relearn who He is. We are in good company with men like David, Moses, Abraham, and Jeremiah.

Read Psalm 46:9-10

      In our homeschool history class we learned that around this time period Assyria was the largest empire on the earth. It was engaged in many schemes of conquest and had already conquered many smaller kingdoms. The children of Israel at this time would have believed that if God would just put a stop to Assyria then He would achieve world peace, and all would be at rest.

What battles are raging in your world that you wish He would cause to cease?

What weapons used against you would you like Him to break and cut in two?

_____

Read Psalm 46:10

Imagine my surprise years later to find "know that I Am" in Scripture. He is the same yesterday, today, and forever. As long as we live He will desire for us to know Him more.

The NASB translation says, "cease *striving*." Maybe your translation says something different. Write it here.

_____

This phrase comes from the transliterated Hebrew word *raphah* which means:

fail, sink, relax, abandon, alone, become helpless, cease, collapse, drawn, fall limp, let go, wait, be still

Do you need to fail at something and just know that He is God? Do you need to relax and know Him? Become helpless so you can receive from the Helper? Cease striving, and allow Him into the situation? I could take each one of these definitions and apply them to my life and my need to "be still" in some area. Can you?

Which one stands out the most? Why?

_____

_____

When I was a kid we had tent revivals every year at our church. One year we had a children's minister come and teach us all the names of God and their meanings. I wish I could remember the name of the minister because the method he used to teach us has stuck with me 20+ years later. So much so, that when I read that word for "cease striving," *raphah,* I immediately recalled that minister saying, "Jehovah Rapha he heal-a my cough-a. He is the God that heals." I thought this was too interesting: the word for "cease striving" and "be still" sound so similar to this attribute of God. I dug a little deeper and sure enough the root word for *raphah* is *rapha* (imagine that?) which means "heal".

Oh, I loved this so much. Take a look at what the Strong's Exhaustive Concordance says:

rapha {raw-faw'}; to mend (by stitching), i.e. (figuratively) to cure –

(cause to) heal, thoroughly make whole, become fresh,

be completely healed, be purified, be repaired

God literally infused the attribute of Himself that is healing into the command to *raphah-be still.* When He said to be still He is saying, "thoroughly be made whole, become fresh, be completely healed, etc. and know that I Am God." He was speaking to the part of Him that is already in you.

Believe that He knows how hard resting is for us. We return to rest by knowing who He is, but we do not really know who He is until we rest. It is an impossible command without Him. Remember, we cannot "try" to rest. It comes when we abide. It is not something that you do. It is a place in Him that you dwell. It is in you. It is in Him. It is where you are when you are in Him.

You could read Psalm 46:10 as "Return to rest and know that I am God," "Remember who I am and return to who you are," and "Let me thoroughly make you whole by healing you, and purifying you so that you may know that I AM GOD." Yes, Lord!

Use any combination of these definitions and write this verse so it applies to where you are right now. Do you need to let go or wait and be silent? Remember who God is? Cease striving? Collapse into His arms? Write it here:

_____

_____

The next part of verse 10 says "to know Him." Psalm 46 gives us several examples of Who He says He is, so we do not need to guess.

Read Psalm 46.

Write down every way the psalmist, together with the Holy Spirit, describes Who God is.

_____

_____

Circle your favorite for today then re-write this statement as a declaration to your soul. For example: "Wait and be still, O my soul, and know that God is your refuge."

_____

_____

The Father knows our every burden and trial. He knows how we strive and struggle and mostly try to do the right thing. He knows when we fail and why and He is not mad at us. He wants us to find rest in Him. Though wars rage around us and against us, He is our stronghold. We must turn to Him to see us through. Sometimes our challenges are not as dramatic as "war." Sometimes it is 6:00 am when I have not had my coffee and my children are already up and fighting and the dog had an accident on the floor, and everyone has needs they expect me to fill RIGHT NOW. This is the moment when my spirit and my soul are at war. This is the moment I must call my soul back to rest and receive every provision from the Lord. I can choose to allow God to infuse that very moment with His presence and His strength and grace. He gives me ideas on how to handle the situation, reminds me to breathe and relax my body so that I do not yell, and gives me courage to have patience and to love in what is literally the mother's darkest hour!

Pray through Psalm 46:

God, You are my refuge and my strength. You are my very present help in times of trouble. Therefore, I will not fear, though the earth should change and the mountains crumble into the sea; though the waters of the earth roar and foam and the mountains quake. Despite every natural disaster there remains a river whose streams make glad the city of God where you dwell. The streams of which are my resting place in You, and You are in the midst of me also, so that I will not be moved. Here I may experience fullness of joy and You will help me. Though the nations uproar and the kingdoms totter, the earth and all the battles raging around me and in me must submit to Your command and the sound of Your voice. You are the Lord of hosts, God with us. Jesus. Immanuel. You are the God of Jacob, our stronghold. You make the wars to cease and it is You who destroys the works and weapons of the enemy. You say to my heart, "Cease striving and know that I am God; I will be exalted among the nations and the earth. I am the God who is with you, the God of Jacob, your stronghold." Father, I receive Your words as truth and know that You are Who You say You are.

Amen

Know That I Am

Lesson 2

Read Genesis 17:1 and write down what God said to Abraham:

_____

     This is one of those verses that at one point in my life would have made me feel guilty. I would have looked at a verse like this, found myself anything but blameless, and would have taken up striving to be better. The problem was not the Bible or even with reading the Bible. The problem was that I already felt unworthy and this verse would have been used as a justification for what I already believed about myself: "I am not good enough." "God could not love me." How can I be in His presence when I am not blameless?"

     The truth is, I did not really know, El Shaddai, the God Almighty. It looks like Abraham did not either because the Lord needed to appear to him and say, "I Am."

Can you imagine the Lord appearing before you and saying that? Read down to verse three and write how Abraham responded:

_____

How do you think you would respond?

_____

     He did not appear as a soft breeze, or a dove, or even a burning bush. This was the Lord, God Almighty appearing before Abraham. And Abraham does not collapse until a whole two verses later which tells me he was not immediately pulverized by the glory of God. But you have to admit, this verse makes God out to sound pretty intimidating. That did not jive well with who God has revealed Himself to me, so I took a deeper look at this verse.

Write down what "Walk before Me, and be blameless," means to you.

___

Because of my personal, psychological bent toward finding myself lacking, when I first read this verse I read it backwards, "be blameless, then walk before me" or "walk before me blameless." I could not have been more wrong. Let me explain why. The short definition for the Hebrew word "halak" translated as "walk" is: *come, to go before, access.*

Take a moment and let the weight of that meaning sink in. Hear Him say, "I am God Almighty, *access* Me." Completely changes the tone of the verse, right? Now read the definition for "blameless" which comes from the transliterated Hebrew word "tamim" and let it set you free: *to be made, or to become complete or finished.*

He is not saying, "Once you become perfect THEN you may enter My holy presence." He says, "Come. I Am God Almighty, access Me for everything you need, and I will make you complete." He *makes* Himself *accessible* so we may be made whole.

Read Psalm 84:11

Write the words used to describe Who God is:

___

Now, knowing what you just learned from the meaning of "walk before Me blameless" from Genesis 17:1 write what you think the phrase "those who walk uprightly" means from Psalm 84:11.

___

___

He is the Lord God. He is the Sun and Shield, the Lord who gives grace and glory. He is God Almighty who does not withhold blamelessness from those who access Him. This is the God we serve. Know Him. We must strip away our cultural connotations to the word "upright", so it does not imply being perfect which leads to guilt or shame. We must view "walking upright" and "walking blameless" to mean that we are choosing to access God. We can choose to access Him and be made complete.

Read through Psalm 84 in its entirety and write down all the ways God is described.

_____

_____

I love the Hebrew word "mishkan" for "dwelling" in verse one. It means *tabernacle, dwelling place, or resting place*. Say yes today to all He has made accessible to you as you pray through Psalm 84 and receive every attribute of God, access Him, and be made complete.

How lovely are Your dwelling places, O Lord of hosts! My soul longs and even yearns for Your courts, the sound of Your trumpets and the sound of Your voice. My heart and my flesh sing for joy to You, the living God. Like a bird when it finds a house or the swallow a nest, my heart finds joy and a home in You, my King and my God. How blessed are those who dwell in Your house. Lord, when I access You I find strength and am blessed. Create in my heart highways that continually access Your presence, that I may be drawn repeatedly to my resting place. Cause my resting place to be a spring of living water and cover me with blessings. Bring me from strength to strength as I access Your presence and my place of rest. O Lord of hosts, hear my prayer; give ear, O God of Jacob! You are my shield, O God. You make my face shine with Your gracious anointing. I would rather stand at the threshold of Your house then dwell in the tents of wickedness for a day in Your presence is better than a thousand elsewhere. You are a sun and shield, I receive the grace You give and trust that you withhold no good thing. You have made Yourself accessible. Make me complete for how blessed the man is who trusts in You. Amen

Know That I Am

Lesson 3

In the last two lessons you learned that God wants you to know that He is I AM. He is the God that sees and knows you on an intimate level while simultaneously, He is the God that sits on the throne and reigns over the universe. He is THE God. Today, I want you to know that He is YOUR God. He says over you, "Know that I Am yours."

Read John 13:1

I talk with women every day who struggle and I, myself, have struggled with letting go of unrealistic ideas of what marriage should look like. Ideas that usually include a prince charming who never gets tired, never has struggles of his own, never makes mistakes, is always romantic, writes love letters, brings home flowers, and most of all never fights with you, and if you have kids he is also the perfect father. I could go on and on. If you have been married, are married, or know anyone who has ever been married then you have probably come to realize that is just not what marriage looks like most of the time. Yet, we still hold on to these fantasies. I know some of you may not be married but this still applies to you because you do not have to be married to have misconceptions about marriage, dating, or men in general.

What I have discovered for myself and have seen in others is that these desires always stem from our justifiable, extremely beautiful need to be completely known and loved by God. We want to be found desirable 100% of the time. We want the fairy tale, "to be loved to the very end". You are not wrong in wanting to be swept off your feet, but Jesus is the One you want. My husband can shine the light of Christ in his love for me. My husband can be an expression of affection from Christ. I love when I see Jesus in my husband. Together, we can show Christ to our kids and those we meet. But, Jesus is the only One that can fill all the empty places of my soul: not my husband, not food, not exercise, not money, not volunteer work, not my church, not my family or my children, not work, not drugs, not my friends, not sex.

Write what you are tempted with most of all to fill any emptiness you may feel.

Jesus loved with a love that was so completely poured out to the very end, but His "end" never ends. He is loving completely right now. The word "end" here in John 13:1 translated from the Greek word "telos" which the NAS Exhaustive Concordance describes as "continually." It is better understood not as a conclusion like, "the end of a story," or as a time in which it will stop but more descriptive of the *amount* of love Jesus has. It is as if Jesus is saying He has loved them and us to the uttermost, in the fullest degree, up to the limit. Can you see Him in the final hour, ready for what was ahead, knowing He had loved them to the fullest degree? He filled their souls to the very brim with His love until they could not contain any more. Being confident of this, He laid His life down for them and for us.

       This is what fairy tales are made of, and it is perfect. He is the One you want. Do not look for that complete love anywhere else because I guarantee you, you will not find it. Our souls find rest in Him alone.

Write about a time when you knew that God was your God or that He showed up in a personal way that ministered just to you. If you cannot think of a time, take a moment and write a prayer asking Him to and believe He will.

_____

_____

If you are married or in any relationship where you have held someone else responsible for unrealistic expectations that only God, the Lover of your soul, can fill write their name down and consider apologizing to them. Take a moment to write a prayer of repentance.

_____

_____

Read Psalms 146

How does David describe God in verse 2?

_____

Who is David talking to in verse 10 when he says, "the Lord will reign forever, Your God, O Zion"? Who is Zion?

Benson's Commentary said this of verse 10: *"The Lord shall reign for ever* — His kingdom shall continue throughout all the revolutions of time, and to the remotest ages of eternity; *even thy God, O Zion, unto all generations* — Christ is set as King on the holy hill of Zion, and His kingdom shall continue in a glory that shall know no period. It cannot be destroyed by an invader: it shall not be left to a successor; either to a succeeding monarch, or to a succeeding monarchy, but shall stand for ever. It is matter of unspeakable comfort that the Lord reigns, as Zion's God, and as Zion's King, that the Messiah is head over all things to the church and will be so while the world stands."

We are of the Church; the Kingdom of Zion and He is our King.

Start in verse 5 of Psalm 146 and list all the ways God is described and all the things He does for you as a member of His kingdom.

It is beyond impossible for any mortal man to fulfill all these amazing things the Lord provides for us. This is why David tells us in verses 2-4 not to trust in man, not princes, and not even Prince Charming. He says this not because we should close our hearts and not trust anyone, but because no one will satisfy us like Jesus. No one can save us like Jesus.

Read Psalm 18:6-17

Do you believe that you serve a God who loves you enough to shake the heavens and the earth to rescue you? Is it bold or presumptuous to believe that the Lover of your soul would be so crazy in love with you that He would move heaven and earth, swoop down on a cherub with wings of wind, raining down hell fire and brimstone, shooting lightning bolts, to deliver you out of the flood and the arms of the enemy? David believed it. He was not ashamed of the confidence he had in his God.

As we pray through Psalm 18, let every possessive pronoun, "my" ring true and clear. Declare that He is your God and your salvation.

I love You, O Lord, my strength. You are my rock and my fortress and my deliverer, my God, my rock, in whom I take refuge; my shield and the horn of my salvation, my stronghold. I call upon the Lord, who is worthy to be praised, and I am saved from my enemies. In my distress I will call upon You, my God for help. When my cry reaches Your ears, I am confident in this: You are moved. You are angry at the injustice I walk through, You are my defender, my Savior. My cry brings me right into Your presence. You caught me, reached all the way from sky to see; You pulled me out of that ocean of hate, that enemy of chaos, the void in which I was drowning. You stand me up in a wide-open field. I stand here saved- surprised to be loved! You light my lamp; The Lord my God illumes my darkness. Your way is blameless, I will follow You. You are my shield and I take refuge in You. Therefore, I will give thanks to You among men, O Lord, and I will sing praises to Your name.

Amen

Know That I Am

Lesson 4

I have a pretty good handle on the fact that God is THE God. He is the God and Creator of the Universe and worthy of my praise and my trust. Got that, (I mean I actually do not even come close to fully understanding that, but I do not struggle agreeing with it or declaring it). Plenty of experiences have led me to a confident understanding that God is MY God. I can claim Him as my own. He is the Lover of my soul and I adore Him. Where I get into the most trouble is knowing that God is the ONLY God. From Him alone comes my salvation. Now do not worry, I am not bowing down to any graven images or anything like that. But, I do sometimes get distracted and forget to put Him first, let my worries or problems take up more space in my heart than my trust in Him, or ignore the leadings of the Holy Spirit out of fear instead of obeying Him out of my love and respect for our relationship.

There are many places in the Old Testament and the New I could reference to show that God is the only God and we are to put Him first. I am not going to do that. I think that if you are doing this study then you probably are well aware that He is the only One we should be serving. I do not want to rain down shame on you and I definitely do not want to use the Bible to do it. I do hope and pray that today's lesson will help you let your soul be reminded to find rest in Him *only*.

Read Psalm 62:1-2

Verse one says, "my soul waits in silence for God only." Is this an area you struggle? Are you ever tempted to turn to other masters to give you rest? I will list a few of mine to help you get started: food, Netflix, worry, busyness (I know it is the opposite of rest but sometimes being busy gives me a rest from whatever it is I wish to avoid), and money. I went straight for the jugular on those because we cannot tip toe around this issue. It is so easy to get distracted or to let the things of this world feed us those temporal highs, so we never have to go deep with God. Deep can be hard. It often is, but going into the deep places of God, with Him, is what this life is really about. It is so easy to let God fall to the background of our lives especially if we are not in crisis. We have to learn to give Him more. The more of us we give the more of Him we receive.

List the things you turn to, to find rest in ways other than in the Lord.

_____

_____

Something interesting I have discovered about the Psalms is that the more David or the other psalmists testify that God is God alone the more they praise Him. The more they praise Him the more confidently they testify that He alone is God. The more they describe Him in spirit and truth the more they praise. The more they praise and worship Him the more they proclaim His character. Do you see how this works? The solution to making Him Lord of your life above all else is to praise Him. The more you talk about Him the more He is magnified in your heart and soul and in your life.

Read Psalm 28:6-9

Do you see the natural progression David's prayer takes? In verse 6 he starts with, "Blessed be the Lord," (He is THE God) then, "The Lord is my strength and my shield; my heart trusts in Him." (He is MY God.) This leads us back to praise when he says, "therefore my heart exults and with my song I shall thank Him." (Praise)

We can use this as a model for bringing God back to the center of our lives when other thoughts and circumstances rise above His throne in our hearts:

Step One. Use your own words to describe God as Alpha and Omega, THE God.

_____

Step Two. Use your own words to describe why God is YOUR God. David was a man of battle so it is natural that he would describe God as being his strength and shield. Who is He to you?

_____

Step Three. After you have meditated on your answers from the two previous questions take a moment and allow the praise to naturally bubble up from your heart.

Write that praise here.

_____

_____

When I find myself wandering far from my place of rest, usually completely broken down and exhausted, I hear His whisper across my heart calling me to *"Remember who I AM."* I am naturally drawn into His presence when I remind my soul of who He is, who He has been to me, and allow myself to praise Him. I picture all my worries and problems as helium balloons, all crowding for the top spot in my soul. When I focus on the Lord, He rises to the top, often popping a few of those balloons on the way up.

I love that the next step in David's prayer here in verse 8 turns into intercession. It is natural for us to be led to intercede for others when God reigns in our hearts. Suddenly, our focus is not on our own little worlds and our own problems. I love that David prayed that God's people would know Him the same way that David had experienced Him. David asked for God to be their strength and shield because that is what he knew. He had seen and experienced God as those things and it was natural to want that for his people. You have to believe that the experiences that have drawn you to the Father allow you to pray for others who need to experience His saving grace in the same way. It is not by accident that I am able to pray for the fatherless in a way that is pure and genuine and brings encouragement. It is because I have experienced the beauty of being transformed from fatherless to a Daughter of the Most High.

Write a prayer for anyone the Spirit brings to your mind. Pray that God would show up to them in the same way He has to you.

_____

_____

Pray through Psalm 63.

O God, You are my God; I will seek You earnestly; my soul thirsts for You, my flesh yearns for You, in a dry and weary land where there is no water. Thus, I have seen You in the sanctuary, to see Your power and Your glory. Because Your lovingkindness is better than life, my lips will praise You. So, I will bless You as long as I live; I will lift up my hands in Your name. My soul is satisfied as with marrow and fatness, and my mouth offers praises with joyful lips. When I remember You on my bed, I meditate on You in the night watches, for You have been my help, and in the shadow of your wings I sing for joy. My soul clings to You; Your right hand upholds me. I will rejoice in You, my God.

Amen

Know That I Am

Lesson 5

I made it to the end of this chapter and struggled with writing this last lesson. I wrote all I wanted to say on this topic in the first four lessons. I went around and round with trying to finish it before I finally stopped and asked the Lord what the last thing was that He wanted me to say about who He is. I heard clearly one word, "Hope."

When I heard that word I immediately felt a weight drop down in my stomach. I sat with it a while, asking the Lord for direction. I realized that usually the only time we start thinking about hope is when we need it. Usually, we only need it when things are bad. We do not often think about hoping in God for the good things to come when things are already good. We do not often admonish our souls to hope in God unless it is already in despair. I have to believe that for Him to speak so clearly to me it must mean many of you need to hear it because you are experiencing a season of hardship. This is the weight I feel.

Read Psalm 42

The *Matthew Henry Concise Commentary* said this of Psalm 42, "Living souls never can take up their rest anywhere short of a living God. When the soul rests on itself, it sinks; if it catches hold on the power and promise of God, the head is kept above the billows. And what is our support under present woes but this, that we shall have comfort in Him."

This psalm to me sounds like it was written by a man who was barely able to keep his head above "the billows". It is generally believed that David wrote this chapter. Personally, I think it sounds like him. It reads like an ocean wave; he is up and then he is down. He tries everything he knows to do: praise, he calls to remembrance the works of the Lord from the past, calls on the name of the Lord, he chides his soul to hope in God; yet, still he ends the psalm in despair.

Read Psalm 42:1 again. Really look at this beautiful psalm.

The transliterated word for "panteth," and in the subscription "brayeth" is "arag" which only occurs here in Psalm 42:1 and in Joel 1:20, where it is used to describe "beasts of the field" "crying" to God in a time of drought. The word means: *to rise, to ascend*; and then: *to look up toward anything, to long for*. It refers here to the intense desire of the hind (or the deer), in the heat of day, for water; or, in Joel, to the desire of the cattle for water in a time of drought. And there is such an idea of tenderness in the Hebrew word "ayyal" for "hart," meaning: *female deer, gazelle*. These animals are so timid, so gentle, so delicate in their physical body. They are a natural object of love and compassion so that our feelings are drawn toward them. We sympathize with them, feel sorry for them. We feel deeply for them when they are hunted and run away in fear. Nothing could more beautifully or appropriately describe the earnest longing of a soul after God, in the circumstances of the psalmist, than this picture.

Have you ever been in such despair, such longing for God to come and rescue you? Have you known that He is THE God, He is YOUR God, He is the God you serve, and yet feel like He is nowhere to be found? Have your "tears been your food day and night" (v3)? Has the enemy fed you lies, "Where is your God" (v3)? Whether due to clinical depression or other mental illness, trauma, or a season of difficult circumstances we all experience times when our souls "become disturbed within" us (v5).

Write about a time when you felt "deep call to deep" when the salty waves of life repeatedly crashed over you and your soul was in despair.

_____

_____

I thought about a season of hopelessness in my life. Compounded with a difficult pregnancy, a hormonal imbalance leading to a diagnosis of depression, and my marriage being in serious trouble I started experiencing suicidal thoughts. I would be driving along with my daughter in the back seat and think about driving off the nearest bridge. This was not me. I have been through hard things, but I had never experienced depression and never had a hard time looking on the bright side of life. During this season I was isolated not being in church, estranged from my family, married to someone with an attachment disorder, taking care of a two-year-old, working nights part time, and extremely sick because of my pregnancy. Needless to say, I was having a hard time looking on the bright side. Thankfully, I had the courage to seek help with my obstetrician who prescribed some medication and therapy sessions with a psychologist. This is where I tell you to seek help with a doctor if you are experiencing depression or suicidal thoughts. It does not make you a bad or faithless Christian to seek medical attention for mental health. In my case, it was the tool Papa used to reach into my life and rescue me.

Read Psalm 42:8-9

Do you see how opposite these two verses are? "The Lord will command His lovingkindness in the day time and sing over me at night," vs "Why have you forgotten me?" Is it possible to feel broken and desperate yet still know that we are loved, that the Father is singing over us?

I love what the author, Wayne Jacobsen says about experiencing seasons of despair and life's barren winters in his book *In Season*, "By allowing us to face the reality of life in this age, He is drawing us to the end of ourselves and more deeply into Himself. There we will learn to rely on Him and His love in ways that will untwist the damage of sin and allow us to be all that He originally created us to be. In the end, that's what makes us truly fulfilled and in turn, fruitful." Knowing these things does not often change our circumstances but it does give us hope.

Read Psalm 130:6-8 and Romans 5:5-8

Write the parallels in these scriptures.

_____

_____

Both make three major points: hope in the Lord, the Lord's lovingkindness, and redemption. Did you also notice that phrase in Psalm 130:6, "My soul waits for the Lord"? All of this happens in our resting place with God. There is a transaction that takes place in our soul when we wait, rest, and hope. He lifts our burdens and pours out His love. All of this is possible because of Christ. I believe that He wants us to know that He's not *just* God. He is a loving Father who sent His Son so we could have hope. When we know Him, we can hope in Him and when we hope in Him we will never be disappointed because it is impossible for Him to fail at loving us.

Pray through Psalm 130 and ask Him for your hope to be restored.

Out of the depths I have cried to You, O Lord. Lord, hear my voice! Let Your ears be attentive to the voice of my supplications. If You, Lord, should mark iniquities, who could stand? But there is forgiveness with You that You may be worshiped. I wait for You, my soul does wait, and in Your word do I hope. My soul waits for You, Lord. It waits and it hopes in You for with You there is loving-kindness. And with You there is abundant redemption. You have redeemed me from all my iniquities.

Amen.

Chapter 3
I Will Complain

Notes:

Small Group Discussion Questions:

1) Share with your group what "complaining" means to you and whether or not it makes you a "bad Christian" to do it.

2) Discuss with your group how the idea that it is OK to complain to God makes you feel.

3) Share with your group any "complaints" you have been holding on to.

4) What are some of the ways you handle your complaints if you do not let God know them?

Chapter 3: I Will Complain

Psalm 121 NASB

1 I will lift up my eyes to the mountains;
 From where shall my help come?

2 My help comes from the LORD,
 Who made heaven and earth.

3 He will not allow your foot to slip;
 He who keeps you will not slumber.

4 Behold, He who keeps Israel
 Will neither slumber nor sleep.

5 The LORD is your keeper;
The LORD is your shade on your right hand.

6 The sun will not smite you by day,
 Nor the moon by night.

7 The LORD will protect you from all evil;
 He will keep your soul.

8 The LORD will guard your going out and your coming in
 From this time forth and forever.

I Will Complain

Lesson 1

One thing I love about David is he was not afraid to express himself to God. He never felt the need to justify his feelings or explain himself or back pedal. Often his psalms seem sort of jumbled up and out of order. I imagine him praying so emphatically and earnestly that the words just flow out however they come like he is thinking or processing out loud with his best friend. He was not afraid to tell God all his grievances, all his worries and concerns, or any of his thoughts on how he believed God should handle the situation. He gripes and complains, is overly dramatic, a roller coaster of emotions, and when he is mad he makes his feelings known. He talked to God the way we talk to our best friends: with freedom. This shows me that God can handle our complaints and our anger towards others and even towards Him.

Read Psalm 55:22

God does not want us to carry any of our burdens. The words "your burden" in this psalm are translated from the Hebrew word *yehab* which means "what was given." I will go ahead and put that definition right into the verse to get a clearer understanding of what David is saying. "Cast your *what was given* upon the Lord and He will sustain you"

Read Matthew 11:28

"Heavy-laden" in the NASB or "burdened" in the NIV are translated from "phortíon" in Greek meaning *a literal or metaphorical burden*. The imagery you get from this definition is that of a shipping vessel loaded down by too much freight.

How would you describe *yehab* from Psalm 55 in laymen's terms?

___

How would you describe *phortíon* from Matthew 11 in laymen's terms?

_____

_____

Take a look at Psalms 55:22 from a little different angle now.

A few definitions from the NAS Concordance of the word "cast" are:

to throw, fling, dropped, hurl, left, risked, snatched,

stretching, threw, throw, throw away, shed, blossom, hurl, pluck

Start at Psalm 55:12 and read until you find out what you think David was given that he considered such a burden that he wanted to hurl it, cast it, or throw it in God's lap?

_____

_____

Has there been a time when you have been hurt by someone or a situation so deeply that you, like David, did not think you could bear it (v12)? Can you write it here?

_____

_____

Have you ever been violated? Deceived with words softer than oil? Ever wanted to hide yourself because of the depth of your pain? Write down what stands out the most.

_____

_____

What if the "what was given" was just the hand you were dealt? Write down a circumstance or situation completely out of your control that is causing you pain.

_____

_____

      What if it did not make you a bad person or even a bad Christian to complain the way David did to God about the people or circumstances that hurt you? What if you could cast the hand that was dealt you back over to Him? He is not offended by our complaints, by our murmuring, or by our whining. He can take it. In fact, He wants to take it from you.

Read Matthew 11:28-30 if you need a reminder.

Look again at the definitions for "cast" that I listed for you. Go back and circle the one you would like to do with your burden, or as many that apply.

      All this complaining and all this murmuring is really just a way of praying and naming these hurts and giving them back to God. What happens when we do not do this? We still end up complaining and aching. Do you vent to a friend? Or worse, stuff those feelings because they make you feel like a bad Christian. We should just forgive and forget right? But instead we stew and get bitter, resentful and just plain ugly. If David could pray that those who hurt him would literally find death deceitfully and go to hell (v15) do you think God can take a little complaining and whining from us?

On that note, let's pray through Psalm 55.

As for me, I shall call upon God, and You, the Lord will save me. Evening and morning and at noon, I will complain and murmur, and You will hear my voice, because you always hear my prayers and because I'm not going to stop praying until you do. Lord, redeem my soul in peace from the battle which is against me and the war that rages inside me over _____ (name the person or situation) strive with me. God, You sit enthroned from old- respond to them who there is no change and do not fear You. I _____ (your word for cast) my _____ (your burden) upon You, Lord and believe that You will sustain me; You will never allow the righteous to be shaken. You, O God, I. Will. Trust in You.

Amen

I Will Complain

Lesson 2

Read Psalm 6 in The Message version as dramatically as you can out loud.

Well, now if that is not the whiniest, complaining prayer I ever heard I do not know what is.

Do you know someone as dramatic as David? Do not be shy, you can list their name here even if it is your own.

Could you imagine praying like this or have you been taught that you are not allowed to voice your grievances toward God?

I was a bit of a talker as a child and was constantly told to be quiet. I always got in trouble at school for talking and was labeled a chatterbox, especially in the third grade. Imagine that! When I heard scriptures like Ecclesiastes 5:2-3 (always in the KJV of course) "Be not rash with thy mouth, and let not thine heart be hasty to utter anything before God: for God is in heaven and thou upon the earth: therefore let thy words be few," it planted all sorts of seeds of doubt in my heart regarding my prayer life. *"It is true that I talked too much, I am annoying, and God apparently does not like that, so He must not like me, and He must not want to hear me jabber, so I should learn to keep my mouth shut."* Pair those thoughts with the last part of that scripture and your third-grade brain crafts the image of the Almighty God seated high on a throne in heaven with a lightning bolt ready to beat down anyone who would dare look up. At least that is the picture that popped into my mind.

This was all so confusing to me as a child because the Papa God of my dreams who whispered in my heart His abiding love for me and His delight in me did not mesh with the image so many adults were portraying. For a long time, I kept those seeds of doubt at bay because the God I knew was not like that at all. He was a kind Papa who called me up to the throne room to sit on His lap all the time! However, entering into adulthood, with life's challenges and disappointments adding up, I began to wonder if there was something to this verse and a few others like it that seemed to be the foundation of the religious views on prayer from my childhood.

Then there is David, a man after God's own heart (and mine too), a man that roared at God. He grumbled, complained, whined, screamed at, and murmured at God. I wonder what David would have to say about Ecclesiastes 5:2.

Read verses Ecclesiastes 5:1-3

I liked what one commentator said about these verses, "What becomes of the enormous percentage of public and private prayers, which are mere repetitions, said because they are the right thing to say, because everybody always has said them, and not because the man praying really wants the things he asks for, or expects to get them any the more for asking? It is the heathen that 'think they shall be heard for much speaking.' We need not to tell our wants in many words to One who knows them altogether, any more than a child needs many when speaking to a father or mother…." * In other words, Ecclesiastes 5:1-3 was written for "the heathen" for those who lacked relationship with God. It is not about the number of words you pray. It is about the quality of your relationship with the Father.

Now stay with me, but these comments are so similar to what another commentator said concerning Matthew 6:7 which I have heard taught similarly out of context.

Read Matthew 6:7 first.

He said, "'Use not vain repetitions,' The words describe only too faithfully the act of prayer when it becomes mechanical. On the other hand, it is clear that the law of Christ does not exclude the iteration of intense emotion. That is not a 'vain repetition;' and in the great crisis of His human life our Lord Himself prayed thrice 'using the same words' (Matthew 26:44)." **

Would you describe David's Psalm in chapter 6 as "vain repetition" or "intense emotion"?

On a scale of 1-10, 10 being a vain, repetitive Pharisee and 1 being passionate, dramatic David rate your prayer life.

Read 1 Thessalonians 5:17-19, how would you explain these verses to a third grader?

Do you think verse 19 references the Holy Spirit or a spirit of enthusiasm?

Have you been holding back in prayer because of fear of disrespecting God with your more than "a few words"? Or maybe because you think your feelings are too stupid or childish that He would not want to hear them or be troubled by them?

Write the subject of those unspoken prayers here.

I love what Oswald Chambers said in *My Utmost for His Highest*, "By means of intercession we understand more and more the way God solves the problems produced in our minds by the conflict of actual facts and our real faith in God." The mind is a tricky thing. Problems often appear greater than they are when we have been turning them over and over in our thoughts. The enemy loves to magnify a problem and cause it to appear larger than it is. Only when we voice these problems are we able to compare them to the truth and see the actual facts. We then begin to filter them through our knowledge, faith, and trust in God. We can see what is real, what is overly dramatic, and how He wants us to respond in faith.

Complaining to God is not about being right and trying to convince Him we are right to feel the way we do. It is about opening a door to allow Him to minister to those complaints that we may have otherwise tried to hide. Hiding them does not make them any less real. I will still grumble and complain on the inside, hold onto resentment, or become bitter. At the same time, He is completely aware of all of this yet will allow me to stew in it until I offer it up to Him.

This time when you pray Psalm 6 do not let your spirit be quenched or pray in vain. Picture in your mind your answer to the previous question. Do not bring these requests to a god on a throne holding a lightning bolt. Bring it before your Papa who is sitting in His favorite lazy boy in the living room waving you over to take His hand.

Please, God, no more yelling, no more trips to the woodshed. Treat me nice, I'm so Starved for affection. Can't you see I'm black-and-blue, beat up badly in bones and soul? My soul is greatly dismayed; God, how long will it take for you to let up? Break in, God, and break up this fight; Return, O Lord, rescue my soul; save me because of Your lovingkindness. I'm no good to you dead, am I? I can't sing in your choir if I'm buried in some tomb! I'm tired of all this- so tired. My bed has been floating forty days and nights on the flood of my tears. My mattress is soaked, soggy with tears. The sockets of my eyes are black holes; nearly blind, I squint and grope. Now, depart from me all you who do evil, for the Lord has heard the voice of my weeping. He has heard my supplication, He receives my prayer. All my enemies will be ashamed and greatly dismayed; they shall turn back, they will suddenly be ashamed.

Amen

* MacLaren's Expositions

** Ellicott's Commentary for English Readers

I Will Complain

Lesson 3

By now I hope you have concluded that complaining can simply be an expression of prayer. I love what Oswald Chambers said in *My Utmost for His Highest* that, "So many of us limit our praying because we are not reckless in our confidence in God. In the eyes of those who do not know God, it is madness to trust Him, but when we pray in the Holy Spirit we begin to realize the resources of God, that He is our perfect heavenly Father, and we are His children."

Read Psalm 62:5-8

What would praying in reckless belief look like for you today? Would it sound like complaining? O anything like David in Psalm 62:5-8?

_____

_____

In verse 8 of Psalm 62 where it says "pour out your heart before Him", the word for "heart" is translated from the Hebrew word "lebab" and can be defined as *your inner self, your mind, your will, your emotions, your memories, your consciousness, your moral character, your intentions and determinations*; basically everything that is in you: the good, the bad, and the ugly.

The Hebrew word "shaphak" for "pour" is similar to the one we learned about in lesson one of this chapter to "cast". David is saying whatever metaphorical action you need to take to get what is in, out: pour, drop, throw, cast; do it. In essence, David is teaching his people to be like Him. He is saying we can trust in God at all times, so much that we can do whatever we need to do to get out what is inside of us and give it to Him. Yes, He is a refuge for us (v8) in the sense that He is a physical and metaphorical place we can run to for safety. But, it is not by accident that in the same verse David says to pour out everything inside you AND God is a refuge. He is also a literal refuge for your deepest thoughts, feelings, hurts, and even complaints. He can keep a secret. Your insides are safe with Him. Let Him carry them.

You want to know of another expression for praying? Groaning. It is used so many times in the Psalms in every translation. Have you ever been so agitated at heart that the only thing to escape your lips is a groan? Have you ever done something so embarrassing you could only close your eyes and groan? Or maybe like a wounded animal the only thing to release the pain in your heart is to let out a growl or a groan. Did you know even these He hears and accepts as prayers?

Read Psalm 38:8-10

The subscription to this psalm in the NASB says, *Prayer of a Suffering Penitent. A Psalm of David, for a memorial.* This psalm is the heart cry of a man who has sinned, who is grieving, and who feels utterly alone and surrounded by opposition.

Have you ever experienced such turmoil all at once? If so write it here.

_____

_____

Many of us may not be able to relate to these experiences. Often the groaning prayer is used to describe extreme circumstances like Psalm 102:19-21.

Read this verse and skim the chapter to list the reason the people were brought to the point of groaning.

_____

_____

Reproach of enemies, cursed by men, feeling abandoned by God, a prisoner doomed to death, loss of physical strength and health. Can you relate to feeling any of these? Which one is the most relevant right now?

___

___

Do you sometimes inwardly groan at yourself? Silently cringe? I realized this is my tendency. I do not always give voice to my inward struggle. I tend to meditate on it and relive the scenario over and over in my mind groaning and wincing at myself in humiliation at my perceived ineptitude. This is what David meant in Psalm 5:1 when he said, "Consider my groaning." Groaning here means my *musing* or *meditation*. Do you think that God would be interested in this type of prayer offering? What if we could give Him even our inward sighing, murmuring, musing, groaning, and moaning?

I want to go back to that Oswald Chambers quote where he said, "when we pray in the Holy Spirit we begin to realize the resources of God."

What do you think he meant by "resources"?

___

___

Read Romans 8:26-27

There is that word *"groaning"* again! This time it is the Holy Spirit Himself groaning on our behalf. When I am able to turn my inward groaning into an outward expression of prayer even if all I can muster is a sigh or a groan then I can know that it is the Spirit Himself prompting me and helping me. It is He who is praying to God for me.

Take a moment to gather your thoughts. Every feeling, person, circumstance, doubt, fear, or feeling of shame that would cause you to inwardly cringe and silently turn from God ask Him to bring to the surface. Take a deep breath and allow the Holy

Spirit to exhale a sigh or a groan through you. I don't mean an *OHM* of New Age meditation or even speaking in tongues. Just allow yourself to exhale all the weight of that inner turmoil, offer it as prayer, and know that you are heard by God.

Now let's pray this prayer from Psalm 5.

Give ear to my words, O Lord, consider my groaning over _____ (this matter). Heed the sound of my cry for help, my King and my God, for to you I pray. In the morning, O Lord, You will hear my voice; in the morning I will order my prayer to You and eagerly wait for Your response. For You are not a God who takes pleasure in wickedness; no evil dwells with You. But as for me, by Your abundant loving-kindness I will enter Your house, at Your holy temple I will bow in reverence for You. O Lord, lead me in Your righteousness because of my foes; make Your Way straight before me. Let me take refuge in You and be glad, let me ever sing for joy; and may you shelter me, because I love Your name and exult in You. For it is You who blesses the righteous man, O Lord, bless me and surround me with favor as with a shield.

Amen

I Will Complain

Lesson 4

In the last three lessons of this chapter I wrote a lot about voicing or praying through complaining and not feeling the need to hide our complaints from God. But He does not want us to stay grumbling and complaining. He does not want us to stay mad or confused or disappointed in Him. "Only in God my soul rests, is silenced, and responds; For from Him comes my salvation." (My personal translation of Psalm 62:1)

When our soul is anything but silent, we can let Him arrest and silence our roaring and complaining soul. He wants this to be our natural response to His salvation, so I want to spend the next couple of lessons talking about what He does with those complaints.

Read Psalm 143: 1-4

There are many times in my life that these words could have been mine. Through difficult seasons in my marriage, painful separations in relationships between friends and family, and walking a journey towards inner healing from my past, I have felt like I was dwelling in dark places. Maybe it is because I am a bit dramatic like David, but I have often felt like my spirit was overwhelmed and my soul was crushed. And why cry out when God surely was not interested in my pain? Can you relate?

Write about a time that caused you to cry out like David in verse 1, "God can you hear me?! Why won't you answer?"

_____

_____

Do you feel or have you ever felt like God found you unworthy of an answer or solution to that heart cry? Like David in verse 2, what makes you feel this way?

_____

_____

Can you remember a time your soul felt so persecuted and under attack by the enemy that you felt crushed like David in verse 3? Write about it here.

_____

_____

Was your spirit overwhelmed and your heart appalled at your circumstances like David in verse 4? Why?

_____

Read Psalm 143:5. What did David do when he felt this way?

_____

_____

      In the spring of 2011, my husband and I separated. After a very difficult first 5 years of marriage, with the help and support of my church, I asked him to leave. This began the hardest trial of my life and a season as a single mom of 3 kids. I felt crushed and attacked from every direction and spent literal hours on my knees in prayer crying out to God to help me. I was only 24 years old at the time. In 2009 I began counseling with the pastor of our new church and rededicated my life to the Lord. It seemed the healthier my inner world became because of my relationship with the Father the more disastrous my outer world got. This culminated to a separation with my husband. So, when I cried out like David, well, I did not feel as if I had too many "days of old" to fall back on for encouragement.

Maybe you are like I was and cannot honestly think of any good times to help you through the bad times. Maybe you have always felt singled out and the hand that has been dealt to you is worse than everyone else's. What then?

I realized I had to make a choice. I could believe the lies of the enemy: that this was it, I was alone and unloved, or I could choose to trust that this is not the end of the story. I chose to believe that I still had so much to be thankful for and that if I trusted Him and, fixed my eyes on things above, I could get through anything. The truth is this life can easily be filled with disappointment. This disappointment can be in others, ourselves, or even God.

Read Psalm 143: 6-9

I did not have a lot of good things to remember and meditate on, so I started asking Him for some and to help me see all the ways He had, in fact, shown up in my life. I had to stretch out my hand to Him (v6) to realize He was already holding me.

Maybe this lesson does not hit home for you because you are like David and can easily call to mind all the Lord has done for you. Either way, list three things that God has done for you that you can meditate on to get you through times of trouble.

1 _____

2 _____

3 _____

I love that David often ends a chapter with a declaration of faith after he has voiced all his doubts and complaints.

What was his declaration of faith in verse 8 and verse 12?

___

___

      Psalm 143 is one of my favorite chapters (I know, I say that about all of them). I love it because I can relate so well to what David is praying but also with how he prays it. He starts off a little doubtful, a little whiney, and telling God all about his problems. Then he blends truth into his prayer like he is reminding himself that God really is loving and good. He asks for help, for deliverance because he knows that God is the only one who can help him, and that God is so capable. He can trust God. Next, David reminds God of who He says He is. He is good. He is righteous. He is loving and kind. Then David declares, almost to himself, that he really does want to serve this God.

      I want to pray like David. I want to be honest about my circumstances and how I feel about them even at the risk of sounding like a complainer. Let's remind ourselves of who God says He is because the more we do, the more we will believe it. We will believe it so much that we will know we can ask Him for help and so we will. Then we will declare that we trust Him to take care of it and we will be free to serve Him.

Pray through Psalm 143:

Hear my prayer, O LORD, give ear to my supplications! Answer me in Your faithfulness, in Your righteousness! And do not enter into judgment with Your servant, for in Your sight no man living is righteous. For the enemy has persecuted my soul; he has crushed my life to the ground; he has made me dwell in dark places, like those who have long been dead. Therefore, my spirit is overwhelmed within me; my heart is appalled within me. I remember the days of old; I meditate on all Your doings; I muse on the work of Your hands. I stretch out my hands to You; my soul longs for You, as a parched land. Answer me quickly, O LORD, my spirit fails; do not hide Your face from me, or I will become like those who go down to the pit. Let me hear Your loving-kindness in the morning; for I trust in You; teach me the way in which I should walk; for to You I lift up my soul. Deliver me, O LORD, from my enemies; I take refuge in You. Teach me to do Your will, for You are my God; let Your good Spirit lead me on level ground. for the sake of Your name, O LORD, revive me. In Your righteousness bring my soul out of trouble. And in Your lovingkindness, cut off my enemies and destroy all those who afflict my soul, for I am Your servant.

Amen

I Will Complain

Lesson 5

In addition to being diagnosed with ADHD, my son is now in the process of being diagnosed with a mood disorder. For the last year he has been going into raging temper tantrums that he is unable to control for 1-3 hours at a time. He is just nine years old. As a mom, this has been absolutely heartbreaking, extremely frustrating, exhausting, and maddening. It has been so hard for me to sympathize with him and have compassion when all I want is for him to just snap out of it and gain self-control sometimes. How do I not take it personally when, often, his anger seems to all be directed towards me? He sits on one side of his bedroom door raging, screaming, crying, throwing things, or hitting the walls while I sit on the other side of the door sobbing and praying and begging God to intervene and to hold my son because I cannot. My pleas for every broken piece in his heart and mind to be healed, every empty place to be filled, and for love and peace to reign seem to go unanswered. And I cannot help but cry, "WHY????"

This behavior was not new, but the reality of these diagnoses was and with them has come not only an identity change for him but for me as well. I am now a special needs mom. I constantly find myself asking, *"Is this my life?"*

Have you ever had a circumstance, or a situation take place that rocked your world and changed or added to your identity? Maybe you got married or became a mom and it was not all you hoped it would be? Maybe you got divorced or suffered a tragic loss of some kind? Write it here.

_____

_____

What do we do at times like these when our world gets turned upside down and everything is now unfamiliar to the point we can no longer even recognize ourselves? How do I surrender these broken pieces of my heart and trust that I will somehow get put back together when I know that no matter what nothing can make it as it was?

My accuser whispers, "How could I possibly complain when others have it so much worse than us? There are starving children in Africa after all. How can I be free to complain about my life? If I admit these painful truths does it not question or doubt God's goodness? To be angry with God when things do not work out according to my expectations makes me a bad Christian. It means I lack faith and therefore, displease God when I complain about my trials and tribulations. I am supposed to rejoice over these things, right?"

Can you relate to any of these questions or feelings? Which one?

___

___

Read Luke 18:1-8

I have heard this parable taught many different ways with many different implications. It is one reason I love scripture so much. It is a living, breathing, life-giving *being* all in Itself. After crying out to God one day while drowning in the emotional storm of my son, I was drawn to this passage. By crying out, I went from drowning to being drawn in.

My heart ached as my Papa poured out His love for me. To imagine hearing Jesus say the words, "Will not God bring about justice for His elect who cry to Him day and night?" The knowledge that my pleas had not exhausted the ears of God filled my emptiness. How much more is He a good, good Father? In that moment God answered my prayers for my son. He did not bring the healing that I asked for but in that moment He answered me by filling *me*. He filled me to overflowing so I could fill the emptiness in my son with my love and compassion.

Like David, I have the tendency to have a lot of surface level frustration, doubts, and fears. My immediate reaction is often to question and complain. But when I choose to release these feelings instead of bottling them I realize that underneath all those complaints is a true bedrock of faith, trust, and hope in the Lover of my soul. If I trust Him enough to cry out to Him I am left secure in my salvation by allowing Him to silence me.

Read Philippians 4:6-7

What word, phrase, or sentence sticks out the most to you and why?

_____

_____

What do you think the difference is between *prayer* and *supplication* in verse 6?

_____

_____

One translation says that *supplication* means to literally beg. Have you found yourself begging God for something recently? What was it about?

_____

When we turn our anxious thoughts into pleas, prayers, begging, complaining, groaning, or roaring how does verse 7 say God responds?

_____

     So many times I have heard these verses used to condemn the thankless complainers. Ladies, can we trust that God understands the complexities of our heart's cry? Do you think it makes me any less thankful for the son that I love with my entire being when I cry out in hopelessness about his behavior that is beyond my control? Of course not! And how much more does my good, good Father know my heart?

Do you think it is possible to beg God and still be thankful?

_____

     It does not make us thankless to have requests and to make them known to God. Many have read these verses like this, "Be anxious for nothing, pray only thanksgiving, and then God will allow you to experience peace." What if we could read it this way from the Message Bible instead, *"Let petitions and praises shape your worries into prayers, letting God know your concerns. Before you know it, a sense of God's wholeness, everything coming together for good, will come and settle you down."*

Read Psalm 12:5

God is always near to the needy. He always responds to the heart cry of His children. David got this. We see it over and over in his psalms.

Read Psalm 91:14-15, 20:6, 38:15 and let your heart take courage.

Go ahead and give this a try while you pray through Psalms 86:

Incline Your ear, O Lord, and answer me; for I am miserable and needy because _____. Preserve my soul, for You are my God. Have mercy on me. I trust in You. Be gracious to me, O Lord, for to You I cry all day long. Make glad the soul of Your servant, for to You, O Lord, I lift up my soul. You are good, and ready to forgive, and abundant in lovingkindness to all who call upon You. Give ear, O Lord, to my prayer; and give heed to the voice of my supplications! In the day of my trouble I shall call upon You, for You will answer me. There is no one like You among the gods, O Lord, nor are there any works like Yours. You are great and do wondrous deeds; You alone are God.

Amen

Chapter 4

Nevertheless

Notes:

Small Group Discussion Questions

1) Find out how many at your table are "glass half full" type people. Discuss whether or not your tendency to look on the bright side is out of religious obligation or just your personality.

2) Is being an optimistic person the same thing as having the "Nevertheless Factor"?

3) Share with your group if there has been a time when a "bad thing" happened that was so bad you could not get to a "nevertheless" statement.

4) Discuss with your group a time recently you may have had a "nevertheless moment" but did not even realize it.

Chapter 4: Nevertheless

Psalm 125 NASB

1 Those who trust in the LORD
Are as Mount Zion, which cannot be moved but abides forever.

2 As the mountains surround Jerusalem,
So the LORD surrounds His people
From this time forth and forever.

3 For the scepter of wickedness shall not rest upon the land of the righteous,
So that the righteous will not put forth their hands to do wrong.

4 Do good, O LORD, to those who are good
And to those who are upright in their hearts.

5 But as for those who turn aside to their crooked ways,
The LORD will lead them away with the doers of iniquity.
Peace be upon Israel.

Nevertheless

Lesson 1

One thing I love about David is that he could always cry out before the Lord, complain, demand vengeance, vent his hopelessness but in the end he was always able to say, "But God."

Read Psalm 9: 6-7

Did you catch the "but"? After every hard thing there is always a "but". Write the hard thing from verse 6 here.

_____

_____

Now write the "but" from verse 7.

_____

_____

Read Psalm 9:18

Have you ever experienced a season of distance from God where you felt forgotten, like your needs are going unnoticed before the Lord, or where you felt weighed down with hopelessness?

Maybe you feel that way now. Write about that here.

_____

_____

We may freely speak our reality with harsh clarity and stark truth yet still maintain the unshakable belief in God's goodness and lovingkindness toward us. I call this the Nevertheless Factor. When your soul cries: airing doubt, fear, pain, and heartache, but your spirit is steadfast and declares the truth, "BUT GOD" you are practicing the Nevertheless Factor. This is what David possessed and it is something we must cultivate and practice if we want to be effective at overcoming the constant attacks of the enemy and the difficulties of this world. We let the enemy win by bottling up all our hurt, doubt, or disappointment and ignoring it or covering it with ridiculous religious euphemisms.

What does a "nevertheless" attitude mean to you?

_____

_____

Read Hebrews 12:1-2

I have come to realize that an attitude of nevertheless means having a heightened awareness of eternity. It does not mean a false sense of reality. Jesus endured the cross because He could see the big picture, but He was not delusional about the difficulty set before Him. We can also endure anything when we fix our eyes on Him.

Would you say this is something you struggle with? If so why?

_____

Where I tend to get into trouble is trying to avoid the negative or hard altogether. *"Nevertheless"* was not in my vocabulary until recently. I would down-play the hard thing, ignore it, bottle it, box it, squash it, and deny it. That works for a little while. Denial is a beautiful place to live for a time but eventually the fantasy comes crashing down causing extreme distress. If you do not acknowledge reality how can you surrender it to God? How then, will you be able to allow Him to invade and bring freedom and healing? We do not have to hide our struggle from God. He wants us to share our reality with Him so we can get to a place of *nevertheless* that draws on His reality and His truth to set us free from our struggle and our pain.

The truth is *everything is subject to change* but if we pretend like everything is fine to begin with we rob ourselves of the freedom He wants to bring to our circumstances. I have seen this time and again in ministering to Christian women and all throughout the Church. We have come to believe that if we acknowledge our pain it somehow makes us a bad or an ungrateful, complaining Christian. This is just simply not true.

Let's see what Job, another guy with the Nevertheless Factor, had to say. Read Job 13:15-16

Job went as far to say that his very salvation came by arguing his ways before God. Now let that sink in and shake things up.

Write the "hard thing" from verse 15 here.

___

Now write the "but God" statement.

___

___

Have you ever felt like arguing your case before God? What would you say?

_____

_____

What if it is actually a manifestation of our freedom, intimacy, and security in our relationship with God to air our grievances? What if we knew there was nothing we could do to make Him mad enough to walk away and leave us? Do you believe that? It has been in the moments of true gut-wrenching railing against God that I have felt the most loved. It has been in these moments that He has placed His hands on my face and held my gaze. He poured out His Spirit, love, and truth into my soul. He is able to do this because this is when all my walls are down, every flood gate is released, and I finally let go. It is when I expose the ugliness of my soul and I realize He does not turn away that I feel the most loved and free. It is then that my soul finds rest.

Please do not misunderstand and think that I mean for us to stay in this place of "fist shaking" at God. I simply mean that until we release our anger, resentment, and disappointment that sometimes flies in the face of every religious rule we have been taught, we will not receive the freedom He wants to give us. In fact, I would go so far as to say that I believe it is impossible to stay in this place because of what God is always able to accomplish with a broken heart.

Try it. Start by telling God about any current struggles you are experiencing whether they are of a sin nature or just a manifestation of living in a fallen world. You will feel the shift when it happens. Once those top layers of lies, complaints, moaning, and groaning have been expelled you will find gold when the truth your spirit has known all along is revealed. Like David it might be, "but I will trust in You" or like Job it might be, "but I will hope in You" or maybe even like me it will be, "nevertheless, I KNOW You are GOOD."

Write your truth statement here:

_____

_____

Now in complete transparency before God pray through Psalm 9.

Nevertheless, I will give thanks to You, Lord with all my heart; I will tell of all Your wonders. I will be glad and exult in You; I will sing praise to Your name, O most High for You are my stronghold, my fortress when I am crushed, afflicted, and oppressed. You are my stronghold in times of trouble. I will put my trust in You, for You, O Lord have not forgotten me. You have not forgotten my cries of affliction. Be gracious to me, O Lord; see my affliction and lift me up. I will rejoice in Your salvation. You know my every need and my hopes in You will not be disappointed.

Amen

Nevertheless

Lesson 2

Read Psalm 31: 10-16

Look at the list of all of David's sorrows just from these verses:

        Grief

        Physical weakness/loss of strength

        Loss of physical health

        Taunted, shamed, scorned by enemies (reproached by adversaries)

        Slandered and gossiped about to friends and neighbors

        Ostracized by his peers (no one wanted to be around him)

        Dismissed and forgotten by his friends

        Felt completely useless to God

        Conspired against by his peers, fear of losing his job (as King)

        Paranoia and fear for his life

Circle the ones you can relate to.

Read verse 14 again and write down the "nevertheless" moment.

_____

_____

There is something especially hurtful about being abandoned or betrayed by your friends. I have experienced this enough to know how heartbreaking it can be. But in David's case, he basically got what he deserved. I do not know how loyal I would be if my friend had another friend assassinated so she could steal that friend's husband. Can you imagine? I would have a hard time sticking with my friend even if she was sorry. Hopefully, you cannot relate to having someone murdered but perhaps you do know what it is like to do something legitimately wrong and either have your friends call you out or cut you off from relationship.

If so, write about it here.

_____

_____

If you know what that is like you know it is a double whammy: the shock and grief of losing your friend(s) combined with the guilt you probably feel for messing up in the first place. How do we get through this? David gives us a beautiful example of this in Psalm 51. We will pray through it at the end of this lesson but first read verse 17.

Read Psalm 51:17

I love The Message Bible's interpretation for this verse, *"Heart-shattered lives ready for love don't for a moment escape God's notice."* David's troubles made him a man of sorrows and he acknowledged that his afflictions were caused by his own sins. His friends could not help him. In fact, they all abandoned him. BUT David trusted in God. His confidence did not fail. He believed that God was his Father and Friend; believed that God was on the throne; believed that God could protect and defend him; and he left himself and his cause with God. He trusted that in circumstances like these there is no other sure refuge BUT God. There is always One who will not leave or forsake us; and the friendship and favor of that One is of more value to us than that of all other beings in the universe combined.

Even in our sin we can have the Nevertheless Factor. Even in our guilt and shame, our loneliness and brokenness we can cry out before God and declare the truth: we are forgiven, rescued, set free, and endlessly loved by our Creator, Father, and Friend.

Pray through Psalm 51.

Be gracious to me, O God, according to Your lovingkindness; according to the greatness of Your compassion blot out my transgressions. Wash me and cleanse me from my sin. Against You, You only, I have sinned and done evil in Your sight, so that You are justified when You speak and blameless when You judge. Behold, You desire truth in the innermost being, and in the hidden part You will make me know wisdom. Enter me, then; conceive a new, true life. Purify me with hyssop, and I shall be clean; wash me and I shall be whiter then snow. God, make a fresh start in me and rescue me from the chaos of my life. Make me to hear joy and gladness. Hide Your face from my sins and blot out all my iniquities. Create in me a clean heart, O God, and renew a steadfast spirit within me. Restore to me the joy of Your salvation and sustain me with a willing spirit. Deliver me from guilt. You are the God of my salvation and I will joyfully sing of Your righteousness; I declare Your praise.

Amen

Nevertheless

Lesson 3

    I will be honest with you. I often err on the side of doubt. I am getting better but I do tend to lean into doubt a bit more often than I do faith. I sometimes question and wonder if I really heard God correctly or when things go wrong I doubt His faithfulness. An embarrassing number of my prayers have started out like Psalm 22:1-2. Go ahead and read those verses and tell me you have never sounded like David.

Read Psalm 22:1-2

    What you see here is the exact opposite of everything we studied in chapter one: Return to Rest. In fact, the word "rest" from that phrase in verse 2, "but I have no rest," literally means *silence, a quiet waiting*. The turmoil of his soul would not allow him to return to rest. I can just picture King David tossing and turning in his bed day and night in anguish, crying out to God.

Have you ever lost sleep over worry, tragedy, or fear? Write about your most recent experience.

_____

_____

    The beautiful thing about the Nevertheless Factor is that it is a wonderful tool against these "no rest" moments. I believe there is even a psychological explanation to this. I will not go too deep because I am not an expert on the brain, but I have learned that our brains have neurological pathways that are literal, tiny paths in our brain. Picture your thoughts like little freight trains.

    Let's say there is a persistent thought like a financial worry, "How will I pay my electric bill?" and that thought races through your brain 100 miles an hour over and over from one location to the next creating a deeper and deeper track. Pretty soon this path becomes the path of least resistance making it even easier for your mind to jump on that train and race through it, like a deep worry rut you get stuck in. You lay down in bed and the instant you close your eyes that worry train starts thundering down the tracks over and over. You toss and turn but you cannot silence it and the more you think on it, well, the more you think on it. This vicious cycle becomes an excellent tool of the enemy to steal our rest.

Ever taken a ride on the How-Will-I-Put-My-Kids-Through-College Express or What-If-It's-Cancer Midnight Freight? If your worry train had a name, what would it be?

___

      Now here is where the Nevertheless Factor comes into play. It is like jumping in front of that speeding train and demanding with the authority of a child of God that it must stop. That train dramatically throws on the breaks and comes to a screeching, crashing halt.

Read Psalm 22:3-5 to see what I mean.

      Round and round David doubts and cries out succumbing to his feelings of abandonment and fear when suddenly the Spirit of Truth rises up and says, "YET You are holy." In other words, "I toss and turn day and night feeling alone and forsaken, nevertheless You are holy, and it is You who sits enthroned. My ancestors have cried out to you for generations. Though I am not getting a response from You now, I know it is in You our fathers trusted and cried out to and You did not disappoint them."

      This is an excellent time to point out that God will often use our past victories to get us through our current trials. And if you do not have any that you can think of you can borrow some of David's and many others from the Bible. David regularly reminds himself and God throughout the psalms of his past victories and of God's faithfulness.

Can you think of a testimony, either yours or that belongs to someone you know, that relates to your current test? Write it here.

___

I wish I could say that that is the end of our troubles but often our thoughts will circle back around to that well-worn path of doubt.

Read Psalm 22:6-19

There are two more clear "nevertheless" moments for David. Find them and write them here.

_____

_____

It is so important that we not overlook this part. Do not fall into guilt and shame over your doubt and unbelief when, after declaring the truth, you hop back on for another restless night aboard that worry train. Call your spirit to attention and declare those nevertheless truths however many times it takes to derail the enemy's lies. It took David three times, but his heart did a complete 180 degree turn.

Read Psalm 22:23-24

David starts this chapter out with "why have You forsaken me" and "I cry, but You do not answer." It is amazing that by the end of this chapter David is encouraging us.

What truths in verse 24 does he give in response to the lies he believed in verse 1 and 2?

_____

_____

Always, God will turn our doubts and unbelief into modes of encouragement for others. It is His own private joke at the enemy's expense. He loves it. This is why our testimonies are so important and encouraging for other Believers. Do not be afraid to share your story even if it starts out with doubt like David's did.

Pray through Psalm 3 and 4

Oh Lord, how my adversaries have increased! Many have risen up against me. (Take a moment and tell God what's worrying you.) Nevertheless, You, O Lord, are a shield about me, my glory, and the One who lifts my head. I cried out and You answered me. I am able to lie down and sleep in rest for You sustain me. I will not be afraid for You have conquered all of my enemies. Oh God of righteousness, answer me when I call. Relieve me in my distress; be gracious to me. I know You hear my prayers. I will meditate on You in my heart while I lie in bed and am still. I will trust in You. You have put gladness in my heart and in peace I will both lie down and sleep, for You alone, O Lord, make me dwell in safety.

Amen

Nevertheless

Lesson 4

In the last three lessons I talked a lot about transparency before God about our struggles and how this vulnerability leads us to our foundational truths. These truths I call "but God" or "nevertheless" statements. We see this over and over again in Scripture. Let's look at another one.

Read Psalm 34:19

Notice that David gives a clear distinction here that these are the sufferings of the righteous. This is important. The righteous suffer from things that the unrighteous do not suffer. We suffer when we see injustice in the world and choices we know are contrary to the will of God. Unbelievers do not suffer in this way. We suffer when the divine order of family is destroyed. We suffer because we see great loss due to sin. So much of our suffering is out of our control and has nothing to do with our own choices. In this way the righteous suffer and in this way we are able to relate to Christ's suffering. The answer to this suffering is the same as Christ's: blessing. God does not repay our sin with suffering and we must not either. We may not condemn or curse. We must bless.

I love what Dietrich Bonhoeffer had to say about this verse in his book *Meditations on Psalms*, "In the suffering of the righteous there is always God's help because he suffers with God. God is always by him. The righteous man finds God in his suffering. That is his help. Find God in your separation and you find your help." Bonhoeffer was a man with the Nevertheless Factor and he defines *blessing* to mean "Nevertheless, you belong to God." When we respond to our suffering with blessing we are walking out the will of the Father.

Take a moment to try and "find God in your suffering." An example of this would be if you are feeling lonely you could write about the loneliness Jesus must have felt before His crucifixion.

Write anything that comes to mind here.

_____

_____

  The ability to say "nevertheless" or "but God" in the middle of our suffering is one thing but how do we deal with the conflicts of this world and the suffering we experience because of them? We do not give up, we do not reject the world, we do not damn it to hell, we do not close ourselves off and despise the unrighteous. We must call these sufferings up and offer them to God. We give them hope by laying our hands on them and blessing them when we say "Nevertheless, you were created by God, you belong to Him, and He is your Creator and Redeemer." This is taking the Nevertheless Factor to a whole new level.

  You may not be directly or physically impacted by the choices of the world, but you feel suffering because of it, nonetheless. Something that causes me deep suffering is the injustice I see towards the poor and homeless in my community.

List a conflict or situation that you know of in this world that causes you heartache.

_____

_____

  My initial response to this kind of suffering is to do one of two things: I take on the weight of the world in my own strength and try to solve all of life's problems with my plans and efforts to fix mankind or I turn a blind eye.

What is your first reaction?

_____

_____

Bonhoeffer purposed a solution to this:

> *"The righteous man must be a blessing, there where he is. God's blessing is the impossible and only by the impossible can the world be renewed."*

There are two vital points in this statement I want to expound on. First, *there where he is*. You do not have to leave your sphere of influence to be a blessing on mankind. Allow the Lord to use you where you are. Inquire of Him for how to do this. Ask how you can hook up with Him to be a blessing where you are now.

The second vital point is that doing this is, in fact, impossible. Being a blessing to those who curse you, being a blessing to those who out right reject God and being a blessing to those who are not even aware they are outside the will of the Father is impossible in our own strength. This is where we see the deliverance of the Lord that David spoke about in Psalm 34:19.

Read Psalm 34:18-19

The Lord is near to the brokenhearted and crushed in spirit. He delivers the righteous man from these sufferings by being present in them. This is when we can say, "though the things of the world crush us, *nevertheless* I bless the world." When the tragedies of this world are brought to your attention trust that it is for a reason. Allow yourself to feel the loss. Do not hide from it. But neither should you dwell on it, allowing it to weigh you down. Allow your heart to break for what breaks His. Then allow Him to bless the world through you.

Read Psalm 41:1-2

What does "considering the helpless" look like to you?

_____

_____

Note the word *consider*. He did not say, "he who helps the helpless," "he who wages war," or "takes up donations." He just said to *consider*. The Strong's Exhaustive

Concordances defines the Hebrew word "sakal" translated to "consider" as: *look at, give attention to, ponder, have insight, comprehend, deal prudently*. It is the same concept we see in the parable of the Good Samaritan. The Good Samaritan considered the helpless man and he acted accordingly.

Sometimes to avoid the pain of suffering and the unrighteous we avoid it all together. We cannot do this. We must consider the helplessness of this world. We can use the Nevertheless Factor to help us with this. What if I could look at the hurting, broken, and homeless man on the street corner and instead of feeling guilty for not picking him up and taking him to a shelter or giving him money, I could bless him? Instead of judging and rebuking him or completely ignoring him I could pray, "*Nevertheless*, despite everything, you belong to God. May God's blessings come upon you, may He renew you and redeem you."

Write a prayer of *nevertheless* here for what brings you suffering.

_____

_____

Psalm 79 is a prayer of dissatisfaction with the way the psalmist's world looked. The NASB subscription for this chapter says, "A Lament over the Destruction of Jerusalem, and Prayer for Help." I do not know about you, but I could certainly lament over our nation.

I am going to take some liberties with today's prayer, but it is based off the sentiment of chapter 79. Consider reading it first for some context.

O God, all around the world Your holy one's are being victimized, brutalized, and martyred. The Church has become a reproach to our culture, a joke and derision to those around us. How long, O Lord will you tarry? Pour out Your Spirit on the nations that refuse to acknowledge You and Your wrath on the kingdoms of darkness encamped against us. Forgive our nation for our sin and the iniquities of our forefathers. Let Your compassion come quickly to meet us for we, Your Church, are brought very low. Help us, O God of our salvation, for the glory of Your name. Deliver us and forgive our sins for Your name's sake. Lord, the unbelievers of our nation mock Your Church and ask, "Where is their God?" Let Your name be known among the nations and that You are our Defender. Let the groaning of the captive, those in prison, and the afflicted come before You; according to the greatness of Your power preserve those who are doomed to die apart from You. Return seven times what the enemy has stolen. We, Your people and the sheep of Your pasture, will give thanks to You forever. We will sing Your praises to our children.

Amen

Nevertheless

Lesson 5

I saved my favorite "nevertheless" statement for last.

Read Romans 8:37 and write it here:

_____

_____

Such a power verse! It is filled with impactful words. Write the one that stands out most to you.

_____

Different words from this verse stand out to me depending on the season I am in. Right now, I love the word *overwhelmingly*. Yes, Jesus. We do not just overcome by the skin of our teeth. We *overwhelmingly* conquer through Jesus. Maybe you liked *all*. As in ALLLLLLLL these things we overwhelmingly conquer. Go back and read verse 35-39 and write down all the "things" listed there:

_____

_____

_____

About 4 summers ago I faced an "all these things" summer:

I was ginormous pregnant with my fifth child (that should count as at least two things)

My husband was working at a job he loved but was way too overqualified and underpaid for (Did I mention we were having our fifth kid, so money was tight?)

Our house was too small for 7 people

Our van was running on nothing but a hope and a prayer

Our medical insurance dropped us unexpectedly (always fun when you are about to give birth)

We were dealing with a major flea infestation that just would not go away no matter what I did thanks to an abandoned house next door with an overgrown yard

Our washer and dryer quit working (from all the washing because of the fleas)

The replacement washer and dryer quit working (not even kidding)

Our vacuum quit working (from all the vacuuming because of the fleas)

Our air conditioner had a mind of its own

Our dishwasher stopped working

My son cracked our glass stove top on accident and broke it

Our hot water heater died

This is the season God started developing in me the Nevertheless Factor. Ladies, I vacuumed every, single day trying to get rid of those fleas. Do you know what it is like to have four kids, three of them boys, and to have to vacuum every day? That means you have to *clean* every day at least enough to see the floor. I washed all of our linens every single day until our washer and dryer *literally* gave out. Then I had to haul all our dirty laundry to various loving, nonjudgmental friends and family who were willing to let me do it at their house. Sometimes I washed them by hand and laid them out to dry on the trampoline in the backyard!

I remember handwashing dishes (in cold water because our water heater was dead) with my daughter who was about nine at the time. I was trying to make light of the situation and told her that her uncle and I had to handwash dishes all the time because we did not even own a dishwasher at the time. I remember her being so sympathetic, giving me a hug, and telling me how sorry she was that I had to endure that! I still chuckle over that.

Keep in mind we were completely broke in this season of life just barely making it pay check to pay check. It was such a mess. I spent many nights sobbing, whether from the frustration and exhaustion, hormones, or self-pity. But, after I cried all the tears I could cry, I would say, "NEVERTHELESS, in all these things we overwhelmingly conquer through You because You love us; I am convinced that NOTHING can separate us from that love!"

Now let me tell you what God did by the end of that summer:

> My husband got a new job and his pick of salary because two companies competed for him which meant over an $11,000 a year raise.
>
> Better insurance because of my husband's new job
>
> A new obstetrician who waved the upfront deposit for no other reason than he just felt he should (over $500)
>
> A gorgeous, brand new washer and dryer completely paid for by our home warranty insurance (it took them 3 months to pay it but they did)
>
> Someone felt led to GIVE us a new fully-loaded SUV
>
> I started a small women's Bible study that eventually grew from three to 28 women that summer
>
> And now I am using all those trials to testify of God's love right now as you read this

His faithfulness is undeniable. Can you see how the season of toil was repositioning our family to receive? If you are going through a season of "all the things" write them here.

_____

_____

Now, go back to Romans 8 and tell your soul and "all those things" the words of verse 28 and 31. Shape these verses into a "nevertheless" statement and write it here.

_____

_____

Read Romans 8:35-37 and write where else in Scripture you think verse 36 written?

_____

How perfect is it that it is from a psalm?! Read Psalm 44:9-22

Why do you think Paul references this verse in his letter to the Romans?

_____

      The psalmist of Psalm 44 sounds a bit confused. If you read the whole chapter it seems he cannot decide if God is really for them or against them. First, God hears their prayers and delivers their fathers. Then God scatters them and afflicts them and by His mighty arm He favors them and gives them victory over their enemies. Yet, God rejected them and abandoned them, made them a reproach and a laughing stock. Finally, in verse 17 the psalmist writes that all these things have come upon them, but they have not forgotten the Lord or deviated from the path the Lord set before them. Then he declares they are as sheep led to the slaughter and because of God they are killed all day long. This chapter made my head spin.

Do you believe it is possible to be conflicted in times such as these; to know in your heart one thing but be tossed back and forth by your circumstances? Write about a time this happened to you.

_____

_____

What do you think Paul could possibly be trying to get at by bringing up this Scripture in his letter to the Romans?

_____

_____

The condition of the saints described in these chapters describe a time when men and women of God were subjected to suffering that was equivalent to dying, sometimes even being condemned to death.

You will see the same sentiment expressed in 1 Corinthians 4:9 as you read it.

And again, as you read Galatians 4:29.

What these 4 passages have in common is what God's faithful people may expect from their enemies at any period when their hatred of righteousness is stirred up. It would be naïve for us to think that we are not in these times now. *NEVERTHELESS, we overwhelmingly conquer through Him. Neither death, nor life, nor angels, nor principalities, nor things present, nor things to come, nor powers, nor height, nor depth, nor any other created thing, will be able to separate us from the love of God, which is in Christ Jesus our Lord.*

Let's pray through Psalm chapter 7, appropriately titled: The Lord Implored to Defend Against the Wicked, and chapter 8.

O Lord my God, in You I take refuge; save me from all those who pursue me and deliver me. If they catch me I am finished: ripped to shreds by foes fierce as lions, dragged into the forest and left unlooked for and unremembered. O let the evil of the wicked come to an end but establish the righteous. You are my shield Who saves. You are a righteous judge, who is indignant over wickedness. You get me ready for life: you probe for soft spots, you knock off our rough edges. You make me safe. I will give thanks to You, Lord, according to Your righteousness and sing praises to the name of the Lord Most High. O Lord, our Lord, how majestic is Your name in all the earth, who have displayed Your splendor above the heavens! From the mouth of infants and nursing babies You have established strength because of Your adversaries, to make the enemy and the revengeful cease. When I consider Your heavens, the work of Your fingers, the moon and the stars, which You have ordained; what is man that You are mindful of him, and the son of man that You care for him? Yet You have made him a little lower than God, and You crown him with glory and majesty! You make him to rule over the works of Your hands; You have put all things under his feet. O Lord, our Lord, how majestic is Your name in all the earth!

Amen

Chapter 5

Teach Me Your Ways

Notes:

Small Group Discussion Questions:

1) Share with your group a time you felt like Jeremiah, unqualified to do the work you knew the Lord was calling you to do.

2) Have you ever been guilty of asking the Lord for the "fruit" of knowing Him without committing to the surrender of relationship?

3) Discuss with your group how the story of Dietrich Bonhoeffer makes you feel and the perspective his life brings to "daily submission to the will of the Father."

Chapter 5: Teach Me Your Ways

Psalm 119:1-10 NASB

1 How blessed are those whose way is blameless,
Who walk in the law of the LORD.

2 How blessed are those who observe His testimonies,
Who seek Him with all their heart.

3 They also do no unrighteousness;
They walk in His ways.

4 You have ordained Your precepts,
That we should keep them diligently.

5 Oh that my ways may be established
To keep Your statutes!

6 Then I shall not be ashamed
When I look upon all Your commandments.

7 I shall give thanks to You with uprightness of heart,
When I learn Your righteous judgments.

8 I shall keep Your statutes;
Do not forsake me utterly!

9 How can a young man keep his way pure?
By keeping it according to Your word.

10 With all my heart I have sought You;
Do not let me wander from Your commandments.

Teach Me Your Ways

Lesson 1

Hello, my name is Katie Holt and I am a recovering people-pleaser, do-er, striver, and try-er. I never want to be found lacking before God or anyone else. I habitually try to make my own heart right before I go before Him in prayer and if I am unable to do so, well then, I often avoid Him. Turns out, it is nearly impossible to avoid the God of the universe who is constantly calling your name.

It is amazing how we try to hide things from Him though. Whether it is sin or our emotions, we often try to keep things from Him, even when we know very well that He knows it all. Since the beginning, in the Garden, mankind has been trying to hide our sin because of shame.

Though my spirit knows that God does not deserve my anger or disappointment, my soul sometimes looks at my circumstances and feels betrayed or unworthy. The next stop on this journey is shame when the truth is God has no expectation for our perfection.

Read Psalm 139: 1-4

I love verse three of Psalm 139: *"He knows our path"*. He knows our past and our journey through it. He knows what we have been up against our whole life and He is intimately acquainted with all of our ways and why we do things. We cannot disappoint Him, and we are never found lacking.

What is the first emotion you feel after reading Psalm 139: 1-4? Does it make you feel comforted or uncomfortable to know He sees it all and knows it all?

Skip down and read verses 23 and 24 of Psalm 139. After the realization that God knew all that was in his heart and mind, what natural response did David have?

He responded with "lead me." There is something so simple and humble about those two words. Knowing that nothing was hidden from God, David humbled himself and responded by asking the Lord to teach him.

I have been surprised to discover just how many times after praying for rest or rescue that David follows these pleas with asking for guidance, to be taught, or to be led by the Lord. Let me show you a few. Read the following scriptures:

Psalm 27: 5, 11

Psalm 86: 7, 11

Psalm 25: 3, 4

Psalm 143: 9, 10

Even Jesus modeled this for us; read Matthew 11: 28, 29.

The hard part for a recovering striver is to not take a phrase like "teach me Your ways" and get overwhelmed or take it on as a burden. The solution is humility. Pride says, "I can handle things on my own. I know what to do. I can fix this." It takes a great deal of humility for a recovering do-er like myself, to allow the Lord to take over, to teach, and to care for me.

I imagine that David was a Grade A Do-er himself. So, it comes as no surprise that he often speaks about the majesty of the Lord, the vastness of His power and supremacy. Recognizing the greatness of God and the smallness of mankind is incredibly humbling and the best way to combat a "do-ing" mentality. It puts all of our puny efforts into perspective. David had a beautifully poetic way of writing about creation and the works of the Lord.

Read Psalm 19:1-7

What would you say is the theme of the first six verses?

___

What is the natural progression of David's prayer after He extols the Lord for His awesome works?

___

David grew up in a world without cell phones or TV or video games. He spent all of his time as a boy in nature witnessing, what I imagine, was breathtaking views and countryside. He spent time cultivating an attitude of humility by recognizing the smallness of his existence compared to the vastness of God's and His creation. Nothing humbles a soul quite like being in nature. I remember as a teenager seeing the Grand Canyon and feeling so tiny in comparison and struck with awe at the majesty of God. In these moments we are given the opportunity to experience God, His creativity, and His power. The only response to this is humility: laying down all we think we know to recognize His supremacy in all things. I can see from the scriptures and my own experiences that He delights in the heart that responds with a willingness and desire to know Him and all His ways.

If you struggle with humility or trusting the infinite wisdom of God in all things, take some time this week to get out in nature. Go on a hike, visit a lake, or even gaze at the stars on a clear night. Be around God's creation and let Him reveal more of His nature to you.

Respond with praying through Psalm 19.

The heavens are telling of Your glory, God; and their expanse is declaring the works of Your hands. Day to day pours forth speech, and night to night reveals knowledge. In them You have placed a tent for the sun, there is no hiding from its heat. The revelation of Your Word is whole and pulls my life together. The signposts of creation are clear and point to You. Your direction is plain and easy. Your decisions are accurate down to the nth degree. Your instruction is perfect. Your commandments are right and pure. They bring joy and enlightenment to my heart. The fear of the Lord is clean, enduring forever. Your judgments are true and completely righteous. I desire Your will above all else. It is more precious than gold and sweeter then honey. Teach me Your ways. Your Word warns me of danger and directs my path. Forgive me for every way I've stepped off that path and keep me from pride and thinking I can take over Your work; I receive Your forgiveness and am made blameless. From now on let the words of my mouth and the meditation of my heart be acceptable in Your sight, O Lord, my Rock and my Redeemer. Amen

Teach Me Your Ways

Lesson 2

Read Psalm 40

So much of this study up to this point could be summed up with this psalm.

Write the words David uses to describe His resting place (verse one and two).

_____

Write the result of seeing and knowing the Great I Am (verse 3).

_____

Find David's complaint and write it here (verse 17).

_____

For bonus points see if you can find David's *nevertheless* moment. Here is a hint, read verse twelve then verse eleven.

_____

In verse eight we see David's heart to know the ways of God. Write what He says about it.

_____

The real point I want to make with this lesson is also found in this chapter of Psalms.

Read Psalm 40: 3-4

It is not by accident that David starts this psalm with rest. He moves to remembering and praising God for what He has done. Then he mentions trust before he ever gets to the Law and the ways of the Lord. Without trust it is impossible to open ourselves up to the knowledge and understanding of His ways. If I do not trust the source of certain information then it stands to reason that I will not believe that information or adopt its principles into my life. Trust is key when it comes to allowing God to speak into your life, mold you, shape your desires, and guide you on the path of righteousness. God is the source of rest. If we are struggling with finding our place of rest in Him it may be a result of our lack of trust.

Follow David's lead and write a Psalm that eventually climaxes with an "I trust in You, God" declaration. To do this, first write your "return to rest" statement. Describe it, tell your soul to go there, or just declare that He is your resting place, or your Rock.

_____

Now, remember something He has done for you in the past and write it here.

_____

_____

Next, write a verse or two of praise.

_____

_____

Are you able to confidently say, "I trust in You, God"? If so, go ahead and boldly declare it and write it here.

_____

My friend, Susan, who was also my pastor and mentor says that it is often much easier to declare our love for God than it is to declare our trust in Him. I find this to be so true. It is one thing to know and love Him as our God but completely different to depend on Him and that love. There is a new depth of vulnerability that comes with trusting God. But these are the places He longs for us to go to. He does not take our openness to His teaching lightly. He does not view our trust in Him as a small thing. He knows and understands the struggle. The problem is if we struggle with trust we will also struggle with obedience. It is not a minor issue. It is a big deal to the Father. He desires for us to trust in Him and He is worthy of it. If any part of you resists trusting in Him allow the Holy Spirit to bring it to the surface.

Write anything that comes to mind that keeps you from being able to honestly say you trust in Him.

_____

_____

Doubt. This is the issue for me. I find myself often doubting and questioning what I think He said, what I think He wants me to do, or even in His love, grace, and mercy. Doubt is a result of a lack of trust. When I find myself in this place of doubt, I ask the Lord to lead me back to my place of rest and reveal any lie of the enemy that I may be believing about His character. I go back to the basics: I go to my resting place, I remember who He is, I praise Him for what He has done, sometimes I complain, and I get down to the very bedrock of my faith where I can boldly declare NEVERTHELESS, I TRUST YOU. It is from this stance that I can seek His will and His ways. A desire springs up inside of me to know Him and to be made holy as He is holy. I think this is what David experienced because in verse eight of Psalm 139 he proclaims, "I delight to do Your will, O my God."

Is doing God's will a delight to you? Or does it feel more like a risk or an obligation? Why?

_____

_____

Ask the Lord to reveal any lie you may be believing that is keeping you from trusting in Him. Write it here.

_____

_____

Now ask Him for the truth. Write it here.

_____

_____

Take a moment to pray through everything that has been brought to your attention by the Holy Spirit. Repent and forgive where necessary. Wrap up your prayer by praying through Psalm 40.

I waited patiently for you Lord and You heard my cry. You brought me out of the pit of destruction, out of the miry clay, and You set my feet upon the rock making my footsteps firm. You put a new song in my mouth, a song of praise I will sing to You always. I have seen and known that You are God. I will put my trust in You. You bless all those who put their trust in You, the humble, and the vulnerable. Many are the wonders in which You have done and Your thoughts toward me. There is none to compare to You. I delight to do Your will, O my God; Your Law is within my heart. Pour out Your compassion on me, Lord. Preserve me with Your truth. My heart has failed me, but You deliver me. You are my help. Let all wo seek You rejoice and be glad in You; let those who love Your salvation say continually, "The Lord be magnified!" Despite my affliction and my needs, You are mindful of me. You are my help and my deliverer. Do not delay, O my God.

Amen

Teach Me Your Ways

Lesson 3

> "No one can say yes to God's ways who has said no to His promises and commandments. Acceptance of the will of God comes in the daily submission under His Word. It may be to us only a slight disobedience, and yet it takes from us that thanks and praise for God's ways that come from the heart. To come under the yoke of Christ is painful and hard if we do it against our will. It is easy and gentle when God has won and conquered the heart."
>
> Dietrich Bonhoeffer from *Meditations on Psalms*

I just love this quote. Bonhoeffer wrote it in reference to the birth of Christ and Psalm 25:10.

Read Psalm 25:10

To learn God's ways, to be taught by Him, to read the Word, to faithfully steward it, does become painful if it does not spring up from an honest, humble spirit of love and affection towards God. We can make the spiritual disciplines of prayer, fasting, and reading the Word a religious, lifeless, and dreaded experience done out of feelings of obligation and a need to perform in order to be made righteous. But that is not what God wants from us when He wants us to submit to His will. We are the ones that miss out when we turn what could be an act of worship into a religious experience or mundane task of mindless obedience or prideful diligence. God is all about relationship. It is why Jesus was born into this world and died for us on the cross. He did this, not so we would feel obligated to read the Bible and pray every day, but for relationship. He wants to win our hearts to Himself and reign victorious over our lives, to bless us, love us, and walk beside us through this life.

Read Psalm 25:8-13

Christ came into this world to save us, to teach us, and to call us to repentance. Bonhoeffer spoke of God's promises. We value a promise by the character of the person that makes it. In the last lesson I wrote how important it is to trust in the character of God. This is so we can depend upon His promises. All the ways of the Lord and all of His promises are lovingkindness and truth. In everything He does we can find His love and grace. When we choose to humble ourselves, distrust ourselves and instead trust in Him, He will be able to guide us in truth. When we choose to follow His guidance and the truth of His Word, we find rest for our souls. Even when we are in pain, physically sick, emotionally distraught, or situationally desperate our soul may be at rest in God.

Read Psalm 25:14

Read Colossians 2:2-4 and write what the "secret of the Lord" from Psalm 25:14 is.

_____

Read Matthew 11:25-26 and write who this secret was revealed to.

_____

Read John 14:23 and write how this secret will be revealed to us.

_____

God "comes unto them and makes his abode with them" (John 14:23), and "teaches them" (John 14:26), and enlightens them, and leads them in His way. The Hebrew word "sod" most often translated as *secret* from Psalm 25:14 can also be defined as, "divan or circle of familiar friends." In a more common tongue, you could say it also means *couch.* It is an intimate whisper shared between just the two close enough to hear it. I just love the idea of cozying up to Papa on the couch so He can whisper to me all of His secrets. It is in this place of resting and abiding that He reveals His ways and teaches us. Notice *sod* does not mean desk, treadmill, or balance beam. It is in this place of abiding love that He reveals Himself, His covenant, and His will. It is not a matter of striving or studying hoping to pass a test.

"He will make them to know His covenant" can be interpreted as *He will make us to clearly understand, to experience, in ever fuller and deeper measure, the meaning and blessedness of His covenant, that is redemption in Christ Jesus.* This is something He does, not something we have to try to do. I am so glad this is not something I have to strive to understand.

It is His responsibility to make Himself known to us. It is our responsibility to seek Him. It is His promise that He will be found by those who do. It is our joy in this life to always search out the great mystery of Christ and our salvation. We will never fully understand all that He has done for us and that is the journey. We are on a life-long treasure hunt of receiving more of ourselves to discover more of Him.

Write a prayer asking the Lord to make the secret of His covenant known to you, for it to be clear, and as simple as if He is speaking to a child.

_____

_____

I know Psalm 119:1-10 is part of your memory work for this study but thankfully there is plenty of Psalm 119 to go around. Let's pray through verses 25-41.

Lord God, revive me according to Your Word. I have prayed to You and told You all about my troubles and You responded. Now teach me Your ways that I may know and understand the deep wisdom of Your precepts. Teach me so I will be able to meditate on Your wonders and be strengthened by Your truth when my soul grieves. Remove any false doctrine far from me and graciously grant me Your truth. I choose You and Your faithful ways. I cling to Your promises, I trust in You. Enlarge my heart to trust You more that I may follow You. Teach me, O Lord, and I will obey. Give me understanding so I can do what You tell me. Make me walk in the right path You lead me on for I delight to walk with You. Cause my heart to turn toward You and be sensitive to Your leading. Revive me in Your ways. Establish Your word to me, as that which produces reverence for You. I long for Your Word, revive me through Your righteousness. May Your loving-kindnesses also come to me, O Lord, so I may know Your salvation according to Your Word. Amen

Teach Me Your Ways

Lesson 4

When I first began reading and studying the Psalms I was immediately drawn to David's psalms, but over time I have really begun to appreciate the Psalms of Asaph.

Read Psalm 77:7-15

In verse two of this psalm he writes, "My soul refused to be comforted." Have you ever felt that way? Have you ever wanted to keep the Lord at an arm's length because you knew you were wrong, and you were not ready to admit it? Or have you felt so grieved and confused by His ways that you did not want to return to rest and receive comfort? Have you felt like Asaph like the Lord had rejected you, failed to meet His promise, or withdrawn His love and grace?

If so, write about it here.

_____

_____

After ten verses of doubt Asaph has his "Know that I Am" moment in verse eleven. Write what he says here.

_____

_____

_____

This leads him to his "Nevertheless" declaration in verse thirteen. Write it here.

___

Somedays no matter how we cry out or if we pray all the right things, we will not get our answer to the problem or find our miracle. In fact, this is often the case. When we finally reach the end of ourselves and our doubt, we must get to a place of accepting that His ways are holy, and His redemption is not to be questioned.

Read Psalm 77:16-20

His ways and His paths are unknown to us. Who can fathom it? Yet we must hold fast to the truth that, though we know not the destination, like a good shepherd He lovingly leads us (v20).

This psalm abruptly ends. Asaph does not expound on how these truths can be applied to whatever circumstances he described at the beginning of the chapter. It is as if just as he begins to meditate on God's holiness and supremacy, he realizes he has made his point. The answer to all these troubles is trusting in God because even though we do not understand His ways He is God. It is as if as soon as Asaph gets to this point, he finds light and joy; his fears suddenly disappear.

I love these words from Matthew Henry's Concise Commentary concerning these verses from Psalm 77: *"The remembrance of the works of God, will be a powerful remedy against distrust of His promise and goodness; for He is God, and changes not. God's ways are like the deep waters, which cannot be fathomed; like the way of a ship, which cannot be tracked. If we have harbored doubtful thoughts, we should, without delay, turn our minds to meditate on that God, who spared not his own Son, but delivered Him up for us all, that with Him, He might freely give us all things."*

Take a moment and write your own psalm acknowledging the works of God in your life. If you have trouble, read through Psalm 77 and borrow one.

___

___

Pray through Psalm 135.

I praise the name of the Lord; I stand in the house of the Lord and praise Your name. I praise You, God for You are good. I sing praises of Your name for it is lovely. You have chosen me for Yourself, for Your own possession. I will praise You for I know You are great and that You are above all other gods. Whatever pleases You, You do, in heaven and in earth, in the seas and in all deeps. You cause the vapor to ascend from the ends of the earth; You make lightning for the rain. You bring forth the wind from Your treasuries. You smote the firstborn of Egypt, both of man and beast. You sent signs and wonders into Egypt upon Pharaoh and all his servants. You smote many nations and slew mighty kings of the Old Testament. You gave their land as a heritage to Israel. Your name, O Lord, is everlasting. Your remembrance, O Lord, throughout all generations. For You have judged me and all Your people with compassion. Blessed be the Lord from Zion, who dwells in Jerusalem. Praise the Lord!

Amen

Teach Me Your Ways

Lesson 5

"Sanctify" is one of those Christianese words I have heard tossed around so much and without thought that it began to lose its meaning. I eventually became extremely uncomfortable hearing words like it. "I don't think that means what you think it means," was always on the tip of my tongue any time I heard someone say it. I finally realized I needed to start over with what I believed and why. The Lord had His work cut out for Him when it comes to repairing the foundational cracks in my belief system. He began to heal and repair and sometimes remove a lot of the principles I had grown to believe.

One thing that has helped me wade through the mire is to treat the Bible as holy and the actual Word of God. I stopped taking it lightly, stopped using Scripture flippantly, and if I do not understand something, I take the time to look it up. All that said, I am not ashamed to admit that after 25 or so years of being a Bible-Believing-Christian that I had to look up the word *sanctify*. I wanted to know if it meant what I thought it meant and if it was really "that big of a deal". Turns out, it is.

Read John 17: 17

Here the Greek word for "sanctify" is "hagiazó" and can be defined as: *I make holy, treat as holy, set apart as holy, hallow, purify.* Huge right? But, can I say that *sanctify* was not the word that blew me away from this verse? No, it was that tiny little word that would normally be completely overlooked between the two weighty words "sanctify" and "truth". It is the word "in," some translations use "by". The value of this little word greatly affects the meaning of the other two. I have always read this verse this way: "Set them apart, make them holy, **with** Your Word of Truth." I have always considered it something like when your filthy with sin the Word washes you clean. But what that little word, "in" means is, "in the realm (sphere) of," more to the point it means the condition (state) in which something operates from the inside (within). So basically "in" means *in* not *with*.

I am sanctified, made pure and holy and set apart, because I am actually *in* the Word or *in* Truth. It is not something that I use to clean up with after I have messed up. It is *where* I am, *in* Him. I guess to me being sanctified always made me feel put out, on the outside of something because I am no longer a part of the world. And while that is true, it is because I am being put *in* something. I am set apart because I am *made a part* of Him.

This understanding is vital when it comes to praying, "Lord, teach me Your ways." My prayer has often been, "Lord, teach me Your ways, help me know Your will, make me holy as You are holy, reveal the truth of who You are to me that I may know You more." Sounds like a good Christian prayer, right? One day the Lord responded and simply said, "Jesus." And I realized that the answer to all my prayers was in that blessed name, Jesus. His Word was made flesh. So, when God speaks, He literally speaks Jesus. Jesus is His verbal and physical answer to every question, every heart cry, every prayer, and every single one of God's ways is Jesus. He is the Way, the Path, the Destination, and the Solution. This is sanctification.

Read Psalm 86:11

That last line, "Unite my heart to fear Your Name," one translation puts it this way, "Unite my soul to stand in awe of You." What if every single part of me, all the hurting pieces, confused places, or even rebellious parts of my soul could be reunited for one singular purpose: to stand before Him in awe? What if every part could surrender to His way, to His truth, and choose to worship? "For Your lovingkindness toward me is great, and You have delivered my soul from the depths of Sheol." (Psalms 86:13)

Is there a part of you that feels *put out* instead of *put in,* like it is not united for a singular purpose of standing in awe of God? Write about it here.

_____

_____

Can you surrender it to Him, knowing that it is already a part of Him? Surrendering to Him does not make what others do or a horrible situation any less wrong. Surrendering is not Him keeping us from something. Surrendering is trusting Him with what is holding us back and receiving from Him whatever He has for us instead. You cannot change people and you cannot control every circumstance, but you can allow the Lord to use those relationships and situations to bring healing, freedom, and maturity in your heart.

Take a moment and write a prayer asking the Lord to sanctify every part of you, allowing Him to receive any part of that refuses to kneel in awe of Him.

_____

_____

Pray through some more of Psalm 119. This is from verses 57-76.

You, O Lord, are my portion. Be gracious to me according to Your promises. I considered all my options and did not delay in choosing Jesus as my way. Morning and night, I will rise to give thanks to You because of Your righteous ways. The earth is full of Your lovingkindness, O Lord; teach me Your statutes. Deal with me according to Your Word. Teach me good discernment and knowledge, for I believe in Your commandments. Once I was afflicted by now, I keep Your word. You are good and do good; teach me Your statutes. With all my heart I will observe Your precepts. I delight in Your truth. Your hands made me and fashioned me; give me understanding, that I may learn Your ways. I will wait for Your word. Comfort me in Your lovingkindness when I am afflicted, and I will trust that You will use every affliction to grow and mature me according to Your word.

Amen

Chapter 6

Contend

Notes:

Small Group Discussion Questions:

1) Discuss with your group how your perspective on the word, "contend" may be different from, "intercession."

2) Share with your group what your "battle" is. Have you felt like you had to fight to feel free, or worthy? Or like you have had to battle for something you have already been given the victory over through Christ?

3) What if you woke up knowing you won? How would it feel? What could you do?

Chapter 6: Contend

Psalm 26:1-11 NASB

1 Vindicate me, O LORD, for I have walked in my integrity,
And I have trusted in the LORD without wavering.

2 Examine me, O LORD, and try me;
Test my mind and my heart.

3 For Your lovingkindness is before my eyes,
And I have walked in Your truth.

4 I do not sit with deceitful men,
Nor will I go with pretenders.

5 I hate the assembly of evildoers,
And I will not sit with the wicked.

6 I shall wash my hands in innocence,
And I will go about Your altar, O LORD,

7 That I may proclaim with the voice of thanksgiving
And declare all Your wonders.

8 O LORD, I love the habitation of Your house
And the place where Your glory dwells.

9 Do not take my soul away along with sinners,
Nor my life with men of bloodshed,

10 In whose hands is a wicked scheme,
And whose right hand is full of bribes.

11 But as for me, I shall walk in my integrity;
Redeem me and be gracious to me.

Contend

Lesson 1

If you have ever spent any time reading the Psalm, then you know you do not have to go very far before you get to David crying out for justice against his enemies. In fact, David often prays for very specific and detailed judgement to be doled out against those who have offended him. Some of his more colorful suggestions on just how God should do this include him asking the Lord for the children of his enemy to become fatherless and his wife a widow! (Ps 109:9) How scandalous would that be in today's Christian church?

How does this line up with what Jesus says in Matthew 5:44 to "love your enemies and pray for those who persecute you"? What Biblical truth can we gain from the prayers for vengeance in the Old Testament that we can use today under the New Covenant of redemption through Jesus? Dietrich Bonhoeffer and Martin Luther believed that the Psalter is both a book of prayer for the Church and the prayer of God. So, are we to believe this applies even to these questionable psalms? In answer to these questions I will quote Bonhoeffer, "The only way to understand the Psalms is on your knees, praying through the words with all your strength. To study [the Psalms] is to make a strange journey of ups and downs, falling and rising, despair and exaltation." I most certainly can testify to this, especially since I began writing this study.

As we work our way through this chapter bear this in mind. When something does not sit well, allow the Holy Spirit to reveal any hidden truths, rearrange your foundational beliefs, or both.

Read Psalm 35:1-10

It is no new thing for the righteous to meet with enemies. Since the Garden, man has encountered an enemy. This continued for David in his trials, Christ in His suffering, the Church in its persecution, and every Christian in our hour of temptation. Our goal for this study is to find our resting place in Christ and stay there. Our goal for this chapter is to allow the Lord to show us how to stay in our resting place despite encountering these enemies of our soul because they are unavoidable.

The Hebrew translation of "without cause" from verse Psalm 35: 7 can be further defined as: *undeservedly, for no purpose.* We have a modern-day translation for enemies like this. The cool kids call these people *Haters*, people who hate on you for no reason.

Have you ever had someone "dig a pit for your soul," set you up, or hate on you for no reason? Write about it here.

_____

_____

Read 1 Samuel 19:1-2

Who was the Hater that David was probably writing about in Psalm 35?

_____

Like David in verse 7 we can feel like we have given our enemies no cause to attack us. This raises even more expectations for God to vindicate us. We must be like David and allow the Lord to encourage our souls and remind us that He is our salvation.

Write what David says in Psalm 35:9.

_____

_____

When we allow the Spirit to bear witness to our spirits that we are saved and that God is our friend, we gain inward comfort for all our outward troubles. This confidence in God is what grounds us and roots us to our resting place so we are not drawn out, ensnared, and trapped by the enemy.

_____

What part of his body does David say cries out to the Lord? Why do you think he uses this part of the body?

_____

_____

What if we believed with all that was within us, with all our strength that the Lord would deliver us? David did. He was convinced the Lord would deliver him.

Many commentators believe a good portion of Psalm 35 is a prophetic foretelling of what is to come for our enemies. We do not get to be the ones that decide on the punishment for our enemies. What a relief! We do get to depend on the Lord for our salvation and the very real judgment that is coming on that great day of the Lord. In this we will never be disappointed.

Pray through Psalm 17

Hear a just cause, O Lord, give heed to my cry; give ear to my prayer, which is not from deceitful lips. You have tried my heart; You have visited me by night; You have tested me, and You find nothing; I have purposed that my mouth will not transgress. I have called upon You, for You will answer me, O God. Incline Your ear to me, hear my speech. Wondrously show Your lovingkindness, O Savior of those who take refuge at Your right hand from those who revolt against them. Keep me as the apple of the eye; hide me in the shadow of Your wings from the wicked who are out to get me, my deadly enemies who surround me. Arise, O Lord, confront him bring him low; deliver my soul from the wicked with Your sword. As for me, I shall behold Your face in righteousness; I will be satisfied with Your likeness when I awake.

Amen

Contend

Lesson 2

We know from Ephesians 6:12 that our struggle is not against flesh and blood but against the forces of darkness that rule in spiritual realms. If I am being truly honest, I cannot think of one physical, flesh and blood enemy that is actively sabotaging my life right now. At one point I would have named a certain elected official or a boss or the mean girls in high school. My point is I do not encounter "enemies" like those in our military who are fighting against real flesh and blood humans. Or the police who fight against "bad guys." Or even David who defeated many armies. Though I currently do not have to separate the face of evil from the face of a person, it is very easy for me to believe Ephesians 6; I know spiritual darkness is real. How do we handle it when there are people in our lives who hurt us? We must recognize they made a choice to agree with the evil one but realize who our struggle is really with. For some it may not be an easy distinction.

David's enemies were clearly defined and many. Without even opening the Bible you can probably think of a few right off the top of your head. List all the ones you can think of.

_____

_____

Read 1 Chronicles 18 and write down a few more you may not have thought of.

_____

_____

It may be easy to think of a few flesh and blood enemies of your nation as well. Go ahead and write down all the enemies of our nation that have risen up in your life time.

You may need a separate sheet of paper!

_____

_____

How do you feel as you write down those names and nations? Do you feel your anxiety go up or your blood start to boil?

_____

Sometimes it can be really hard to strip away the human "mask" of the enemy. It feels unfair, like we are letting the person off the hook for very real choices they made. I find the easiest way to "unveil" the evil one is to forgive the person in agreement with him. For example: when our car was broken into, we felt extremely violated, a little fearful, and angry at the expense of all the damage. I ranted, "How could someone be so thoughtless and destructive? We did not even have anything worth stealing. How could someone rob a person who has FIVE car seats in their car? Who does that?"

It was not until I forgave the person who broke into our car that I was able to expose the real thief. If we continue to throw stones, harbor resentment against, or place judgment on those that hurt us then the real enemy of our souls is not exposed. He is allowed to continue to wreak havoc in our lives.

This is not intended to be a chapter on forgiveness but if we do not understand how this system works, we will continue to spin our wheels, falling right into the enemy's trap. We must expose him in the light of God's truth.

Write down who our real enemy is from Ephesians 6:12.

_____

Write down what Ephesians 6:13 says we are supposed to do about our enemy.

_____

Even David had to learn this. Unfortunately, it may have taken him having to hide out in a cave to fully understand it.

Read Psalm 57: 1-7

In verse 4 David says his soul is among lions. Who does Peter compare to a lion in 1 Peter 5:8?

I love verse one of Psalm 57, "In the shadow of Your wings I will take refuge until destruction passes by." Like Paul says in Ephesians 6:13, David had to put on the armor of God. In his case that looked like standing down and making God his refuge. In other words, we duck and cover in the shelter of the Most High and we wait out the inevitable destruction of our enemy. How can I allow God to contend for me if I am contending for me? How can I allow Him to fight my battles if I am in the midst of the fray? James 4:7-8 says to resist the enemy and he will flee and instead draw near to God.

Take a moment and pray. Ask the Lord to reveal anyone you have targeted as an enemy that He may want you to release so that the true enemy working in your life may be exposed. Forgive where necessary and write it here.

Please know I do not take this lightly. As someone who has spent YEARS prayerfully working out forgiveness towards those who have wounded me, I understand the struggle. This is meant to simply be an exercise or a small step towards allowing the Lord to bring healing and freedom to our souls. It is in our resting place with Him that He is able to accomplish all of these things. So, allow Him to do the heavy lifting and bring forgiveness in your daily bread portion.

Pray through Psalm 57

Be gracious to me, O God, be gracious to me, for my soul takes refuge in You; and in the shadow of Your wings I will take refuge until destruction passes by. I will cry to You, God Most High, who accomplishes all things for me. You will send from heaven and save me; You reproach the evil one who tramples me. You will send forth Your lovingkindness and truth. My soul is among lions who are wild. Their teeth are lances and arrows, their tongues are sharp daggers. Be exalted above the heavens, O God; let Your glory be above all the earth. They have prepared a net for my steps; my soul is bowed down; they dug a pit before me; they themselves have fallen into the midst of it. My heart is steadfast, O God, my heart is steadfast; I will sing, yes, I will sing praises! Awake, my glory! Awake, harp and lyre! I will awaken the dawn. I will give thanks to You, O Lord, among the peoples; I will sing praises to You among the nations. For Your lovingkindness is great to the heavens and Your truth to the clouds. Be exalted above the heavens, O God; let Your glory be above all the earth.

Amen

Contend

Lesson 3

"Betrayal" may be a better name for this lesson's title. Have you ever felt betrayed? Does a particular situation or person come to mind when I ask that question? If so, you are not alone. David knew exactly what it was like to feel betrayed.

Read Psalm 54.

The subscription for chapter 54 in the NASB says this," For the choir director; on stringed instruments. A Maskil of David, when the Ziphites came and said to Saul, 'Is not David hiding himself among us?'"

Read 1 Samuel 23:14-15 and 19-20 to find out who the Ziphites were.

I wish every Psalm was like 54 in that we can know exactly what was going on and what inspired David to write it. Somehow, David learned that the Ziphites, the countrymen of Ziph who were also sons of Judah, betrayed him to Saul. If you feel inclined you can read a few more chapters of 1 Samuel, namely 22-26, to learn more about what a devastating blow this was for David. I love what Psalm 54 adds to the story in 1 Samuel: David's feelings and emotions.

Based on this new information, who were the "strangers" and the "violent men" David mentions in Psalm 54:3?

_____

Read 1 Samuel 23:26-28 then describe how the Lord saved David from Saul.

_____

Who does David give the credit for his escape? (Psalm 54:4)

David's thoughts and feelings did not stop at just giving God credit for saving his life.

Read Psalm 54:5-7

David trusted God with retribution or the recompense of his enemies. This is the step I was missing for so much of my life. It is one thing to pray for salvation from our enemies or our betrayers and recognize that He is our Savior and our Help which we see in Psalm 54:1-4. It is another thing altogether to trust Him with the punishment of those who have wounded us (v5-7). I went most of my life struggling to forgive despite knowing it was the right thing to do. I felt if I forgave, it suddenly let that person completely off the hook. Even after I received much deeper revelation on forgiveness that set me free in so many ways: that it is for us, that it does not obligate us to relationship to that person, and that it is a command (read: gift) that God gives us to set us free; somewhere I still struggled with a deep seeded belief that when I forgave them I was setting them free of all the consequences of their actions. That is just not the truth.

A sin against His beloved is a sin against Him. He holds the bill. We can forgive them but it does not pay the bill. The truth is there is judgment, vindication, and recompense for evil and there will be a day of judgment. This can still be confusing because when we are on the other side of the situation, when we are the perpetrators, we ask for forgiveness. We find it such a relief to our souls to know that instantly we are forgiven. Even those who have wounded us are afforded this same redemption. We do not get to decide how God sets us free. The point is recognizing that it is He who sets us free and we can trust Him with it.

The problem with not getting this is that when we feel we have some measure of control over redemption and judgement we may hold back from forgiveness altogether if we are not ready to let the other person off the hook. We have no control over whether or not that person is on or off the hook. The only control we have is whether or not we want to choose to walk in forgiveness as His forgiven and in the freedom forgiving others brings us. Recognizing that God is our Contender, our Defender, our Righteous Judge, and our Redeemer set me free to fully release the ones who wounded me and to trust Him completely with their punishment. Whatever that may be is really none of my business.

Before you pray through Psalm 54 take a moment to ask the Holy Spirit to reveal anyone you are harboring unforgiveness towards. Write any names down He brings to mind.

Save me, O God, by Your name, and vindicate me by Your power. Hear my prayer, O God; give ear to the words of my mouth. For strangers have risen against me and violent men have sought my life; they have not set God before them. Behold, God, You are my Helper; You are the sustainer of my soul. I trust You will recompense the evil to my foes; destroy them with Your faithfulness. Willingly I will sacrifice to You; I will worship and give thanks to Your name, O Lord, for You are so good. For He has delivered me from all trouble, and my eye has looked with satisfaction upon my enemies.

Amen

Contend

Lesson 4

In the last lesson of this chapter you read about one of the many times David was betrayed and how he responded. We can look to this example and see what can be expected from anyone who has not set God before them (Psalm 54:3). We can also look to Jesus as an example for how to handle betrayal.

Read Matthew 26:47-56

It is a heart-breaking moment in our Lord's story. I cringe every time I read it, especially that last line of verse 56.

Write what it says here.

_____

Has there ever been a time when you felt completely abandoned by friends and/or family? Write about it here.

_____

_____

Read Psalm 56: 8 and write how the words make you feel?

_____

_____

In ministering to women who feel all alone in their circumstances, abandoned, or who are in crisis I find that many take the most comfort from the realization that God is keeping an account of their pain and their tears. Personally, I find I just want to be seen and heard by God and know that He is for me. Of course, I would not mind a rescue and a million dollars while we are at it, but the truth that I am not alone is always enough to see me through. I think the same could be said for David.

Psalm 56:9 says, "God is for me." The word used to describe the Lord, "God" is translated from the Hebrew word "Elohim." This is the attribute of God that is Judge, Divine Majesty, Power, and Ruler.

Write David's prayer from Psalm 7:8

_____

_____

Remember Psalm 54:1 from the previous lesson? Write it here.

_____

_____

David repeatedly prayed, asking the Lord to contend for him and to vindicate him throughout the Psalms. These words all have the same implication, that there is a supernatural courtroom and God is our divine judge.

Read Psalm 43:1

David pleads his case and prays that the Lord would deliver him. How do we apply this to our lives today and the betrayals we face?

Read John 8:36 and write it here.

_____

We are free. The Judge has already cleared our name. We have already won against our accuser.

Remember as you pray through Psalm 56 or any psalm that may not apply to your current circumstances that you are also interceding for the church, with Christ.

> *Be gracious to me, O God, for man has trampled upon me; Fighting all day long he oppresses me. My foes have trampled upon me all day long, for they are many who fight proudly against me. When I am afraid, I will put my trust in You. In You, whose word I praise, In God I have put my trust; I shall not be afraid. What can mere man do to me? All day long they distort my words; All their thoughts are against me for evil. They attack, they lurk, they watch my steps, as they have waited to take my life. Because of wickedness, cast them forth, in anger put down the peoples, O God! You have taken account of my wanderings; put my tears in Your bottle. Are they not in Your book? Then my enemies will turn back in the day when I call; this I know, that God is for me. In God, whose word I praise, in the Lord, whose word I praise, in You I have put my trust, I shall not be afraid. What can man do to me? Your vows are binding upon me, O God; I will render thank offerings to You. For You have delivered my soul from death, indeed my feet from stumbling, so that I may walk before God in the light of the living.*
>
> *Amen*

Contend

Lesson 5

Recently I watched a video that grabbed my attention when I heard the speaker mentioned the word "contend" because I happened to be writing this chapter at the time. They were saying that Scripture says, God contends with those who contend against you. They went on to say that anytime Christians step out in faith to do the will of the Father or to walk out His calling the enemy will put a target on your back and start causing storms in your life by attacking you. She said we should expect the storms anytime we try to do what is right, but it is OK because we can trust that God is contending for us.

I realize that this has become a fundamental belief in the Church, and it is not the first time I have heard it. But I just cannot get behind an idea that says anytime we are obedient we will be set up to attract the enemy's attacks. What I believe Jesus exemplified is that when He calls us, He equips us, He protects us, and He intercedes for us. The truth is that what we should expect when we step out in faith to do the will of the Father is His covering, protection, and intercession.

Read John 17:9-12

Before Jesus was crucified, He prayed and asked the Lord to keep His disciples from the evil one (v15). He did not ask for all things to be a bed of roses with no trials or troubles. In fact, He was very clear about the many hardships that could be expected by those who follow Him.

Read John 17:15

What I did find in Scripture is that being obedient is not what draws the enemy's attention. That happens the moment we accept Christ as our Savior.

Read 1 Peter 5:8-9

Just like any truth, the enemy takes it and twists it. Being a follower of Christ is not easy and we can expect trials and persecution. The enemy twists this truth into, "The moment we act on our Christian faith we can expect trials and persecution." This makes us think twice about doing His will and stepping out in faith even if only subconsciously. But Peter tells us that all we must do is resist him, firm in our faith, knowing that we are not alone because every other Christian around the world experiences the same suffering.

The Lord gave me a revelation about this one day after talking to my friend who trains horses. Having owned a horse in the past we were sharing funny stories about how fearful horses can be. You let your horse walk around a puddle one time, and they will never again walk through a puddle because of how afraid they will be of water. My friend was in the process of training a horse that had become scared of small dogs. Imagine a giant animal like a horse being scared of a ten-pound dog! She was saying that the way to train a horse to not be afraid is to force the animal to turn and face the dog. The next thing she said dropped into my spirit like a ton of bricks, "You have to show a horse that they are bigger than a dog because they just don't realize it. You have to force them to confront it."

This reminded me of James 4:7. Go ahead and read it.

I began to see the places the enemy had been nipping at my heels and causing me to be fearful. I had always run because I did not know any different. I was believing the lie that my fears were bigger than me.

Are you experiencing any "nips" or attacks from the enemy that have you running? Write about it here.

_____

_____

"Anthistémi," the Greek word for "resist" simply means *to hold one's ground, to not be moved.* It does not mean to fight back or push or come against. Interestingly, it means completely opposite of the word "submit" from the beginning of the verse which means, *bend.*

Only when I *bend* my spirit, soul, and body to the will of the Father am I able to *stand my ground* against the enemy and his fear tactics. When I lose ground because of attacks from the enemy it is not because I am being obedient. It is not a sign that I am doing the Lord's will and am finally on the right path. It is a sign that I need to submit myself to God and resist the enemy's advances.

How much bolder would you be in obedience to the Father and His plan for your if you realized how big you were compared to the pint-sized devil and his schemes? Explain.

_____

_____

Keep these truths in mind as you pray through Psalm 43 and 71.

Contend for me, O God, and plead my case against the evil one; deliver me from the deceitful and unjust! For You are the God of my strength. So why do I go mourning because of the oppression of the enemy? O send out Your light and Your truth, let them lead me; let them bring me to Your holy hill and Your dwelling places. Then I will go to the altar of God for You are my exceeding joy; I will praise You, my God. Why are you afraid and in despair, O my soul? Hope in God, for I shall again praise Him, the Help of my countenance and my God. In You, O Lord, I have taken refuge. In Your righteousness deliver me and rescue me; incline Your ear to me and save me. Be to me a rock of habitation to which I may continually come; You have given commandment to save me, for You are my rock and my fortress. Rescue me, O my God, out of the hand of the wicked, out of the grasp of the wrongdoer and ruthless. For You are my hope.

Amen

Chapter 7
Light Up My Darkness

Notes:

Small Group Discussion Questions:

1) Discuss with your group which season of life you are currently in.

2) Encourage each other with any relevant New or Old Testament Bible stories.

3) What would it mean for you if you could stay in your place of rest despite the season you are in knowing that it will not last forever?

Chapter 7: Light Up My Darkness

Psalm 111: 1-5 NASB

*1 Praise the LORD! I will give thanks to the LORD with all my heart,
In the company of the upright and in the assembly.*

*2 Great are the works of the LORD;
They are studied by all who delight in them.*

*3 Splendid and majestic is His work,
And His righteousness endures forever.*

*4 He has made His wonders to be remembered;
The LORD is gracious and compassionate.*

*5 He has given food to those who fear Him;
He will remember His covenant forever.*

Light Up My Darkness

Lesson 1

Like David, we all experience seasons of darkness in our lives. The question for this chapter is, how do we stay in rest or return to rest in these times? Truthfully, I believe there are a lot of ways we can partner with God to allow Him to shine His light. We can seek professional help, spend time in nature, spend time alone, spend time with friends, volunteer, make physical changes to our diet and exercise, worship, pray, read the Bible, etc.. But what I have found is that it is only the faithful hand of God that can bring us through no matter what we do or try. He is faithful. We can do all we know to do and still struggle with depression or unfortunate circumstances that are outside of our control. What then?

I have experienced one such season. My whole life up to that point I had believed in God and His love for me. Looking back now I see how the circumstances of my life set me up at a cross roads. I had never really been pushed to make a choice to "take up my cross and follow Him." At the time my husband and I had been married a couple of years, we had a toddler and I had just found out I was pregnant with our second baby. I was working nights so we would not have to put our daughter in daycare. It was extremely, physically challenging for me to be up all night and up most of the day with my daughter on top of being exhausted from pregnancy. In addition to these challenges I felt isolated and alone without many friends. My husband and I had spent the first year or two of our marriage arguing every Sunday about which church to go to and why we did not like the other's choice. Eventually, to avoid the argument, we quit going altogether. All of my young, single friends had moved on early on in my marriage because of the different paths our lives had taken. Compound all of these circumstances with the fact that I had also just had a major falling out with all of my family. I felt completely alone. My husband and I were struggling in every sense of the word and life was just overall really hard. My second pregnancy was extremely difficult. I was horrendously sick for the first five months, feeling motion sickness from the second I woke until the moment I drifted off to sleep.

Is my story beginning to remind you of a difficult season in your life? If so, write about it here.

_____

_____

All of these struggles led me to feel doubt in the existence of God. I felt that if He was real then He must not really love me. I was alone. I entered a really dark season of depression and even experienced suicidal thoughts. Thankfully, I was able to voice some of my feelings to my husband which prompted him to schedule an immediate appointment with my OBGYN who prescribed some antidepressants and counseling.

I followed my doctor's recommendations, my morning sickness eventually lessened so I was able to eat again, and I quit my job so I could have regular sleep hours. While all of these outward changes helped, they did not answer my inward questions of doubt about God.

Read Psalm 139:23-24

I really believe the Lord allowed me to struggle a bit in this time of my life, groping and fumbling my way through the darkness, so He could shake up my foundational belief system. It was like every weak area: everything I believed just because that is how I was raised, and every lie of the enemy that I believed was put under pressure. All of this began to be exposed through my questioning and seeking answers. This was the "try me and know my anxious thoughts" part of my story. God knew them already, but I needed to know them.

When David says, "see if there be any hurtful way in me," I do not believe he meant just ways that he hurts other people. I think he also meant any thoughts and beliefs that were being used to hurt himself.

Looking back on your life, write about a time you know the Lord was at work even though things were hard, and you may not have realized it at the time.

_____

_____

Read Psalm 139: 9-12

      Many times, I felt overwhelmed by my darkness but, like David, I can now say that even then the darkness was not dark to God. The next part of my story still amazes me. I was introduced to my husband's friend's neighbor who was an immediate kindred spirit. At a time when I could not receive the love of the Father, He sent me a friend.

Have you ever had a friend who was used by God to love you or help you in some way? Write their name here.

_____

      This friend of mine introduced me to their church and her pastor who began to meet with me for counseling and prayer. This set me down my freedom road and I have never looked back. Through inner healing prayer I discovered that God not only existed, but that He loved me, and had been with me all along. I discovered the root to my fears was tied to childhood trauma I had ignored and been in denial about. The Lord gave me a dream of walking beside Him as a small child, holding His hand, feeling loved, secure, and safe.

I think David had a similar experience because after talking about his darkness in Psalm 139 read what he says in verse 13 and write it here.

_____

_____

Have you ever had an experience like that or received a word from someone that made you feel the love of the Father? Write about it here.

_____

_____

When these seasons of darkness come, and they do for all of us, we must choose to put our hope in Him, trust that though He may feel far He never leaves us and believe that He will bring us through it. It is only a season and, "even there [His] hand will lead me, and [His] right hand will lay hold of me" (Psalm 139:10).

If this lesson is tugging at your heart because you are in the midst of a dark place take a moment and remind your soul that even in the darkness He is there. Ask the Lord to shine His light and illuminate your darkness with His love and truth as you pray through Psalm 139. It is a bit longer but, the affirmation to your soul will be so worth it.

Pray passionately while you connect with the words.

O Lord, You have searched me and known me. You know when I sit down and when I rise up; you understand my thoughts from afar. You scrutinize my path and my lying down and are intimately acquainted with all my ways. Even before there is a word on my tongue, behold, O Lord, You know it all. You have enclosed me behind and before and laid Your hand upon me. Such knowledge is too wonderful for me; it is too high, I cannot attain to it. Where can I go from Your Spirit? Or where can I flee from Your presence? If I ascend to heaven, You are there; if I make my bed in Sheol, behold You are there. If I take the wings of the dawn, if I dwell in the remotest part of the sea, even there Your hand will lead me, and Your right hand will lay hold of me. When I feel the darkness overwhelming me and the light around me is night, I will remember that even the darkness is not dark to You and the night is as bright as day. Darkness and light are alike to You. For You formed my inward parts; You wove me in my mother's womb. I will give thanks to You, for I am fearfully and wonderfully made; wonderful are Your works, and my souls knows it very well. My frame was not hidden from You when I was made in secret and skillfully wrought in the depths of the earth. Your eyes have seen my unformed substance; and in Your book were written the days that were ordained for me, when as yet there was not one of them. How precious also are Your thoughts to me, O God! How vast is the sum of them! If I should count them, they would outnumber the sand. When I awake, I am still with You. Search me, O God, and know my heart; try me and know my anxious thoughts; and see if there be any hurtful way in me and lead me in the everlasting way.

Amen

Light Up My Darkness

Lesson 2

I want to share with you another dark season of my life and how the Lord brought me through it. After several very difficult years of marriage the Lord finally released my husband and me to separate. With the help and support of our church, family, and professional counselors we separated. It was the best decision for our family, but it was absolutely the hardest season of our lives thus far.

I want to be vulnerable with you and share part of my journal from this time in my life:

I am in a season of waiting. I would not have said that before. I thought I was in transition, that I was transitioning from one season to another and just stuck in the middle. I realized today that it feels as if I am in transition only because I have not wanted to accept the new season that I am in. I am in a season of waiting, not waiting to transition to a new season. I have wanted this period of waiting to end. I have wanted it only to be a short period of transition into a new and wonderful season. I have even been so helpful as to suggest to the Lord many fine alternatives to this waiting. But as this realization that this is where I am supposed to be, where He wants me to be began to bloom in my mind the Lord asked me how long I wanted this season to take. If I was going to keep fighting it or if I would choose to **rest in the waiting**.

Rest in the waiting.

Read Psalm 27:13-14

If you are reading in the NASB your translation says, "*I would have despaired* unless..." Write what you think the word "despaired" means.

_____

In the Interlinear Bible this verse is better translated, "Unless I had believed..." A common interpretation of this verse is that by an effort of faith (belief) David was able to pull himself up out of despair by assuring himself that he would, in fact, see "the goodness of the Lord." I believe this to be true.

However, what I love about this verse is a definition from the Strong's Exhaustive Concordance. It says that the words, "I had believed" in Hebrew mean, *to foster as a parent or nurse; to go to the right hand.* Remember from the last lesson, I said that there are many ways to encourage our souls to lift the weight of darkness and partner with the Lord to receive His light? And that sometimes it is only the loving hand of our Parent God that fosters us? He bolsters our hopes and strengthens our souls and bodies; He establishes us at His right hand. Perhaps David was able to pull himself up out of despair by his faith. What this Scripture could also be saying is that if David had not been "fostered," "nursed," or held by the right hand of the Father he would have remained hopeless.

When we begin to put our faith in what we believe our faith can do for us instead of putting our faith in the ability and goodness of God to rescue us from the pit, pull us by His side, and teach us His ways, we have made our faith an idol, friends.

Immediately following in verse 14 it says, "Wait for the Lord; Be strong and let your heart take courage; Yes, wait for the Lord."

What does Psalm 27 verses 13 and 14 have to do with each other? What does God's goodness and my hope in His goodness have to do with waiting?

I think He knows waiting is hard. We have no concept of what *everlasting* or *eternal* means. We only understand one concept of time. That is why He reminds us of His goodness and His everlasting-ness. That is why David had to tell his soul to take courage. It is not our natural inclination to want to wait.

I finished my journal entry with this personal affirmation and it still encourages my soul today. You can borrow it. Go ahead and declare it out loud.

I am loved by an everlasting, good God. Today I will set my hope on Him. I will tell my heart to take courage. I will draw near to Him with a sincere heart in full assurance of faith by letting my Spirit minister to my soul for my heart is sprinkled clean from an evil conscience and my body washed with pure water. I will hold fast the confession of that hope without wavering, for He who promised is faithful (Heb 10:22-23). I will choose to rest in the waiting.

Shortly after I received His word to rest in the waiting, I began to accept a little more each day the fact that I actually had very little control of what He was doing in my marriage. I had to trust Him.

Write down any areas of your life that you now recognize the need to relinquish control over, trust Him with, and rest in the waiting?

_____

_____

Let me encourage you by telling you what the Lord was able to do in my marriage once I started resting.

About five months into our separation I was standing in worship in my living room; our three kids were with my husband. Suddenly, I had a picture, like a movie, play in my mind. It was of my husband and me dancing in my living room. I froze. I became really angry. The pain of longing that vision caused me was extreme. I thought, *"The Lord had to have known how impossible it was for something like that to happen was. Is this a trick?"* Never in my life had my husband danced with me, not even at our wedding! I cried out to the Lord with my disappointment and heart ache. Eventually, I pushed the thought away and went on with my day.

That evening my husband brought our children home. We argued. I do not even remember what we argued about. I told him to lock up on his way out after putting the children to bed, and I disappeared to my bedroom. Behind tears and my bed covers I began to hear music coming from downstairs. I heard a knock at my door and then footsteps. With what I can only assume was an incredibly confused look on my face I asked him just what he thought he was doing while he pulled my arms around his neck and began to sway. I realized he was dancing with me! I think the Lord laughed until He fell off the throne at my incredulity over the situation.

The Lord was not being cruel by giving me that vision. He was proving to me that He was working behind the scenes and that He was trustworthy. He was working on my husband's heart, healing him and making him whole. It was not much longer after that He brought restoration to our marriage and my husband moved back home.

Two kids later I can promise you God is the God of miracles. Your family and your heart are a priority to Him.

Let your heart take courage as you pray through Psalm 22. If parts of it, like the first verse, do not apply to you remember that a Believer out there somewhere does feel forsaken. Intercede on their behalf.

My God, my God, why have you forsaken me? Far from deliverance are the words of my groaning. O my God, I cry by day, but You do not answer; and by night, but I have no rest. Yet, You are holy, O You who are enthroned upon the praises of Your Church. Be not far from me now when trouble is near; for there is none else to help. I am poured out like water, and all my bones are out of joint. My heart is like wax; it is melted within me. My strength is dried up like sunbaked clay. But You, O Lord, be not far off; O You my help, hasten to my assistance. Deliver my soul, save me from the lion's mouth. I will tell of Your name to my brethren; in the midst of the assembly I will praise You. You have not despised me in my affliction nor hidden Your face from me. You heard me when I cried for help. All the ends of the earth will remember and turn to You and worship before You. For the kingdom is the Lord's and He rules over it.

Amen

Light Up My Darkness

Lesson 3

We had just moved into a beautiful new house, something I had been dreaming of for a long time. My husband had just received a raise, so we were financially more secure than we had ever been. After a brief separation and years of counseling our marriage was healthier than it had ever been and getting better every day. All the things that in the past had given me a lot of stress were gone. Yet, I still had this feeling I could not shake. I had all the things, why was I unhappy? Something had been stirring in my inner world for a long time. It was as if the healthier my outer world became the more obvious my inner turmoil. This boiled over one day in the grocery store when suddenly, for no obvious reason, I could not hold back the tears. I made it to my car, and I sat in the parking lot while sorrow filled me, and tears started streaming. I felt the crushing weight of hopelessness and an overwhelming feeling I could not describe. Then His whisper came, "Do not let your heart be troubled. I am the Way, the Truth, and the Life." This both comforted me and confused me.

I felt comforted by His voice and His presence, but the words did not seem to apply. I have often pondered them from John 14 wondering why He said it the way He did: the way, the truth, the life. Do they all mean the same? Was He just trying to drive the point home or are they each significant and different in their own way?

Write what you think each word means.

_____

_____

In a moment of clarity, I heard Him say over me and over us, "I Am always the Way, I Am the Mode of Transportation, the Path, the Direction, and the Destination. When you feel lost, I Am always the Truth; it is a gift I freely give. It sets you free and will always keep you steadfast. When you feel hopeless and weary from the journey remember that I Am Life. I am endless. I am a deep, deep well of resources. I will always satisfy. I Am Light and redeeming Love. So do not let your heart be troubled. Remember who I Am and choose Me."

What I did not realize at the time was that this word was His way of letting me know I was about to enter a new season in my life, a season of silence. In lesson one I wrote about a season of darkness, of fumbling through life feeling lost and unloved, and not hearing even a distant voice of the Lord. In lesson two I shared how the Lord encouraged me through a difficult season of darkness by anchoring me to Himself and strengthening me along the way.

There is a difference between being in a dark silent room feeling completely alone and being in a room full of light, sitting at the feet of a silent Father. I had spent the last ten plus years hearing from God just about every day, feeling His whispers across my heart, and being overwhelmed by His words. Now, suddenly for the first time He was silent. Why would He not tell me the answers to my questions?

My attitude towards the Father became aloof. If He was going to be distant, I could be distant. I was angry.

Throughout this study I have shared a lot with you about the emotional healing of my past through inner healing prayer and counseling. It was a long, hard, yet glorious road of deliverance and freedom. I would not change a thing about it. But I most certainly did not want to relive it. I had my healing, I had arrived, or so I thought. I have shared with you how much growth and healing my husband and our marriage has had over the years. It was as if all my issues were hiding behind the very real and very large challenges he and our marriage had faced. The healthier they got, the more those challenges shrank, the more exposed my issues became and the more I realized I had not, in fact, "arrived" much to my chagrin. Frankly, I was angry about it.

Have you ever been angry with God? Write about it here.

_____

_____

For me, this season of darkness was one of my own making. I refused to even acknowledge the wounds of my past that still hurt me. If it is possible to pretend away your pain, Lord knows, I would have been the one to figure it out because I tried harder than anyone. Sisters, that is just not how freedom works. Allowing the Lord to expose those wounded, hurting places and acknowledging them as real and valid is the only way for them to be healed.

The Lord did not leave me. He reminded me He was the Way, the Truth, and the Life and then He remained silent, in a sense He chose to rest in the waiting until I was ready to receive the healing He so desperately wanted to give me.

Read Psalm 27:8-9

I have always read this verse as David saying to the Lord, "Do not hide your face from me. Do not turn your servant away in anger." I could see how at different times in David's life He felt like the Lord was angry with him or he felt like the Lord had turned away from him. But there is another perspective here the Lord used to encourage me. Sometimes, He turns my words back on me. I think He can do that with Scripture too.

Read Luke 22: 27

Who is The Servant?

Read Hebrews 2: 16-18

Who is our Help?

David described the Lord as saying, "Seek my face," in Psalm 27:8 and he responds, "Your face, O Lord I seek." Then we lose the quotation marks, but the dialogue continues if only in David's heart. This is the part the Lord turned back around on me as if He were saying to me, "Seek My face, do not turn your face from Me. Do not turn your Servant away in anger. I am your Help."

Often what we accuse people of is the very thing we are guilty of ourselves. When the Lord showed me this it was at a time when I was accusing Him of abandoning me and turning from me like David (v9).

Do you have an accusation in your heart towards God? Write it here.

_____

      It was as if in that moment He put His hand on my face, as He does for all of you now, and breathed truth into my soul when He said, "Do not turn Me away. I Am your Help."

      We turn away from Him in anger because we feel He has hurt us in some way. He cannot hurt us. That is an accusation. The truth is He is our Help. The Servant Jesus laid down His life for you. It is an act of humble submission to turn our faces back toward God and receive from Him just as it was for Peter to sit and allow Jesus to serve him by washing his feet.

Let Him wash yours as you pray through Psalm 30 and allow the Holy Spirit to minister any help your spirit needs.

O Lord my God, I cried to You for help, and You healed me. O Lord, You have brought up my soul from death. You have kept me alive, that I would not go down to the pit. I will sing praises to You and give thanks to Your holy name. Weeping may last for the night, but a shout of joy comes in the morning. I have prayed, "Hear, O Lord, and be gracious to me; be my Helper." You have turned my mourning into dancing. You have loosed my mourning clothes and dressed me in gladness that my soul may sing praise to You and not be silent. O Lord my God, I will give thanks to You forever.

Amen

Light Up My Darkness

Lesson 4

"Save me, O God, for the waters have threatened my life. I have sunk in deep mire, and there is no foothold; I have come into deep waters, and a flood overflows me. I am weary with my crying; my throat is parched; my eyes fail while I wait for my God." (Psalm 69:1-3)

There is nothing quite like depression to make you feel like you are drowning. Except maybe financial hardship. Or having a sick child. Or loss of your own personal health. Or a troubled marriage. Or childhood trauma. In other words, there are lots of reasons to feel as if you are drowning. Many of us have probably felt like David here in Psalm 69. You are not alone.

I am no stranger to the feeling that comes when you can barely breathe for the weight of circumstances crashing down on you. David's words so poetically describe how many of us feel in seasons of struggle. When you think you cannot bare just one more thing, one more mechanical problem with your car, or one more bill you know you cannot pay.

"Answer me with Your saving truth," David says. "Deliver me from the mire and do not let me sink." (Psalm 69:13-14)

Do you feel like you are sinking? Share why.

_____

_____

Oh, how David's prayer has mirrored so many of my own. "Can you not see that I am drowning, Lord…" in heartache, financial burdens, relational strain, "answer me! Save me! Why does it seem like You are helping everyone but me?!"

It is beautiful to me that through his drowning, heartache David encourages us.

Read what he says to do at the end of Psalm 69:32 and write it here.

_____

In the NASB it says to "let your heart revive." Have you ever felt like a part of your heart has broken into a million pieces or just completely died? That word "revive" is translated from the Hebrew word "chayah" which means *to let live.* It is the same word used in the prayer of another King of Israel.

Read Isaiah 38: 9-20.

Did you catch the word "chayah"? It was there in verse 16. "O restore me to health and let me *live!*"

These eleven verses bring tears to my eyes because I so relate to King Hezekiah in this prayer. Do you? Have you ever felt deprived (v10)? Have you struggled with sickness and disease to the point you have been unable to be with friends and neighbors (v11)? Have you ever been able to compose yourself for a time, act or feel normal, only to feel completely undone and at the end of yourself no matter what you do (v13)? Have you felt oppressed by the enemy, afraid, or unsafe (v14)? Maybe you have felt like somehow you brought this suffering on yourself, that the Lord was punishing you (v15)? Has your soul ever felt embittered or in absolute anguish (v15)?

Write down any part of his prayer that you relate to or may have ever prayed.

_____

_____

You see Hezekiah's prayer start to shift in verse 17. This verse is a bit confusing, but most commentators agree that what he is saying is that God used his sickness and worked all things together for his good. I loved what Benson's Commentary says, "*My great bitterness was unto peace,* that is, became the occasion of my safety and comfort, for it drove me to prayer, and prayer prevailed with God for a gracious answer, and the prolonging of my life."

I know from experience that the last thing that many of us want to hear is that God is somehow using the "hard" for our good. The Truth is like that sometimes: hard to hear and receive but we must allow this truth to set us free even in our darkest seasons of life.

You know at this point you have to reread Romans 8:28.

The same God who gave His own Son over to death so that our very hearts could be revived. He is the One that does the reviving. Jesus is the living God who once was dead but was raised. It is literally in His nature, the very business of God, to bring what was dead back to life.

David says to us who seek God, "let your heart revive." As you pray through Psalm 118 allow every darkened, broken, hurting, striving, dying place to return to its place of rest in Christ. "For the Lord hears the needy and does not despise those in captivity." (Psalm 69:32-33)

I will give thanks to You; Lord for You are good. Your lovingkindness is everlasting. Oh, let us say, "His lovingkindness is everlasting." From my distress I call upon You, Lord and I know You will answer me and set me in a large place. You are for me; I will not fear. What can man do to me? I take refuge in You because I can trust You when all else fails. When I feel surrounded, I will call upon Your name. When I feel as if I am falling, I will call upon Your name for You are my help. You are my strength and my song. You are my salvation. Joy and salvation are for me, one of the righteous. I will not die, but live, and tell of the works of the Lord that is working all things together for good. I shall enter through the gates of righteousness and give thanks to the Lord for You have answered me and become my salvation. The stone which the builders rejected has become the chief corner stone. This is Your doing; O Lord and it is marvelous. This is the day which You have made, and I will rejoice and be glad in it. Save me and send prosperity. You are God and have given me light. You are my God and I extol You. I give thanks to You for You are good and Your loving-kindness is everlasting. Amen

Light Up My Darkness

Lesson 5

I have touched briefly on Psalm 27 throughout this chapter, but I would be remiss if I did not have you read it in its entirety. It is a beautiful psalm, poetically written, relatable on many levels, and perfectly conveys what I want to say in this chapter. I love the subscription in the NASB for this psalm which says, "A Psalm of Fearless Trust in God."

Go ahead and read Psalm 27 now.

On a scale of 1 to 10, ten being fearless trust and one being no trust at all, rate your level of trust in God.

_____

Write whether or not you feel your level of trust in God has gone up while doing this study guide and why.

_____

_____

Now read Psalm 27.

Why do you think, "they" titled this Psalm 27 "A Psalm of Fearless Trust in God"?

_____

_____

I think I could write a summary of this study guide using only Psalm 27. It has everything. Write the verse(s) which give you the idea David is in his resting place.

_____

_____

I love the description of the Lord's character by David. Write his responses to the Lord's call to "Know that I AM."

_____

_____

David even gives us an example of "complaining" to God. Write it here. (I will give you a hint. It is in verse 10.)

_____

_____

Write David's "Nevertheless" declaration(s) here.

_____

_____

Are you beginning to see any similarities between this study guide and this chapter? If you have not yet, write down verse 11 here and the chapter of this study guide it coincides with.

_____

Write the verses where you see David realize the Lord is contending for him.

_____

_____

Now write where you see that despite all the darkness in his life David is living in the Light (these verses may read a lot like "rest" which is kind of the point).

_____

_____

We have made it full circle back to this chapter. I asked before why you thought Psalm 27 was described as the "Psalm of Fearless Trust in God." I think it is because living these six principals: abiding in rest, knowing the truth about God's character, going to Him with your complaints, declaring "Nevertheless" despite those complaints, humbling yourself enough to want to be taught His ways, and allowing Him to contend for you all require one thing. TRUST.

Sometimes the best way to see if something fits is to try it on. Read through this list of "Trust Statements" and circle any that feel like swimsuit shopping in the middle of January.

I will choose to abide in my resting place instead of trying to fix the problem, worry about the problem, or be in fear over the problem because I can trust the Lord to be in control of it and provide me with all I need. I am safe, secure, and satisfied in His presence so I will stay there. "I will let my heart take courage and wait on the Lord."

I will trust in the goodness of the Lord. He is the defense of my life, so I do not need to fear. He is my Help, so I do not have to live this life alone out of my own strength. When I feel forsaken, even by my own parents, I can trust that He will take me up and love me because He is a good Father.

I can trust the Lord with my crying out and the heartache of my soul. I can tell Him anything from the childish complaints and the selfish longings to the true anguish I feel over injustice in the world and my circumstances because He is safe. He never turns away, always brings healing, truth, and light to my heart when I open up to Him.

I can always get to a place of declaring, "Nevertheless I will trust in You," because no matter what the circumstances You are worthy of my trust.

I can lay down my desires and what I think I know, my plans, and my expectations for how things should be because I trust Your ways are so much higher and better than mine. I would rather know Your ways, O Lord, because they lead me on a level path, and I trust You will not deliver me over to the evil one.

I can trust the Lord to fight my battles and contend for my heart and soul for in the day of trouble He will conceal me in His tabernacle, the secret place of His tent. In my resting place in Him He will hide me. He will lift me up on a rock and my head will be above the enemy.

He is the Light of my salvation. I will trust Him with my heart so even in the darkest seasons of this life I know that the dark is not dark to Him. I am not alone and do not fear. I will wait on the Lord and take courage because I trust Him to see me through.

How did that feel? I hope by now, on your last lesson of the last chapter of this study guide those statements feel a little more comfortable than they would have when you started. If anything did not sit well the best thing to do is take it to the Lord. If after a while you feel stuck, you can redo the corresponding chapter in this study guide, pray and read through the Psalms that correspond, or seek counseling or inner healing prayer. All that to say, you do not have to stay there in that place of lack of trust. My prayer is that every hurting, broken, darkened, dying, or just plain tired part of your soul would be lifted by the Light of the Lord and transitioned into a place of rest in Him.

Let's end this study guide with a bang. Pray through Psalm 27 and allow the Holy Spirit to minister to you in every way only He knows how to do.

You, O Lord, are my light and my salvation; whom shall I fear? You are the defense of my life; whom shall I dread? When evildoer come upon me to devour me those adversaries and the evil one will stumble and fall. Even when I am surrounded on all side by darkness, my heart will not fear. Though war arise against me, nevertheless I will be confident. I will trust. This one thing I ask You Lord, the one thing I seek above all: that I may dwell in Your presence, my resting place, all the days of my life to behold the beauty of my Lord and meditate in Your temple. For in the day of trouble You will conceal me in this secret hiding place of rest in You. You will lift me up on a rock so my head will be lifted up above the enemy. I will offer sacrifices of my own desires with shouts of joy. I will sing praises to You, I praise You, O Lord. Hear me when I cry and be gracious to me and answer me. Teach me Your way, O Lord, and lead me in a level path. I would have despaired unless I had believed that I would see Your goodness. I will choose to wait. I will tell my soul to take courage and wait on You, Lord.

Amen

A Note for Bible Study Leaders:

    This study is formatted to be a seven-week course with a video message to be played each week after discussing the homework and fellowship. I have found that an hour of discussion time for a group of four to five women is ideal. If your group is larger than that you may want to split into smaller groups to allow a deeper connection and intimacy. After discussion time you may want to play the video. There are three to four discussion questions you or the table leaders may want to ask in each group. Be sure and save some time at the end to pray together or read over the next Memory Chapter of the Psalms.

    In my time as a Bible study leader I have found this order of events to be the most fruitful in our time together. However, there is freedom with this study to order things in a way that best suits your needs.

    Thank you for choosing this study and trusting me with your group of women. I promise you I do not take it lightly. I want you to know that I am earnestly praying for you and your ladies that you all may come to a deeper place in rest, relationship, and trust with Papa.

    Grace and Peace,

    Katie Holt

Made in the USA
San Bernardino, CA
11 January 2020